To Eoghan
With Best
from all at
Portree High
June 2011.

D0188252

a year in the life of **the isle of skye** bill birkett

a year in the life of
the isle of skye
bill birkett

FRANCES LINCOLN

Past, present and future: to all those who love Skye

Acknowledgements

Special thanks to my family for some wonderful times on Skye –
Sue my wife (particularly for editing the first draft), Rowan my
daughter, William my son.

To my great friends on Skye who have provided unbelievable
support and encouragement, particularly Fiona Fraser, Ross Cowie and
Tommy Mackenzie. All at the Tongadale Hotel and Pier Bar in Portree.
Thanks to Bill Cowie, property manager on the Isle of Rona (those
wishing to stay on Rona should contact Bill for information, tel. 07775
593055, email ronalodge@tiscali.co.uk). Thanks to Dan Corrigal who
operates the MV *Stardust*, which acts as the ferry to Rona, and also
sealife tours out of Portree (he can be telephoned on 077987 43858).

In particular, to those who have spent so much special time with
me on the hills and wild places of Skye: Dave Birkett, Andrew Sheehan
for his company and knowledge of flora and fauna, John Hargreaves
and the late Freddy Snallam. And to the many climbers with whom I
have shared unforgettable Skye experiences: John Adams, Alan Hinkes,
Mary Jenner, Heather Johnston, Charlie Leventon, Dave Lyle, Alastair
Lee, Duncan Richards, Nigel Robinson (Yorkie), George Sharpe, Alan
Steele, Luke Steer, Mark Squires, Chris Thorpe, Tom Walkington, Bob
Wightman, John White.

To all the local climbers whose words, images and guidance
have been inspirational, particularly Cubby Cuthbertson, Ed Grindley,
Kev Howett, Mark Hunter, Hamish MacInnes, Patsy Walsh and Noel
Williams.

To all those missing, the many friends and climbing companions
with whom I've shared days on Skye – my apologies.

To Martin Bagness for drawing the excellent map.

To Jackie Fay, Librarian at Kendal Mountaineering Reference
Library, Jane Renouf at Ambleside Library, and all at Cumbria County
Council Libraries.

To Anquet Mapping for supplying me with their excellent
computer map information: 1:50,000 Landranger Maps to the
whole of Britain, all on one DVD, which runs seamlessly.

To the best nature/ plant website I have ever seen:
Carl Farmer's www.plant-identification.co.uk/skye/index.htm.

To John Nicoll of Frances Lincoln Limited, who encouraged me to
take on this project and has faith enough to publish my work. To Jane
Havell, who took on the massive volume of material I supplied her
with and shaped it into this special book.

To those protective bodies and groups who care about Skye and
seek to protect its unique character: John Muir Trust, National Trust for
Scotland, Scottish Mountaineering Club, Royal Society for Protection
of Birds, Mountaineering Council of Scotland, Jensen Foundation
(restoration and management of Rona), Scottish Natural Heritage,
Scottish Wildlife Trust (Skye Branch).

To the many who keep reading my books, enjoy my imagery and
buy my prints, talk to me on the fells, and send me informative emails
and letters: thanks for your opinions and knowledge, which are of
great value to me.

Bill Birkett Photo Library

Bill Birkett has an extensive photographic library covering all of
Britain's mountains and wild places. For photographic commissions,
information, prints or library images, telephone 015394 37420,
mobile 07789 304949, or e-mail bill.birkett1@btopenworld.com.
Website www.billbirkett.co.uk includes regularly updated images.

*TITLE PAGE: Rocks and evening reflections looking south-east from
the head of Loch Coruisk towards Sgurr na Stri. Remote Coruisk, a
valley of rock, lies at the wild heart of the Black Cuillin, enclosed by
great heights of jagged gabbro mountains. On this spring evening
of rare perfection, awesomely quiet with hardly a breath of wind
(and, in April, too early for midges), I slept out on the greensward
between the shingle beach and the heather: I can think of no finer
night among mountains, even though my bag was white with frost
the next morning. The sea inlet of Loch Scavaig lies, unseen, through
the notch in the hills.*

Frances Lincoln Limited
4 Torriano Mews
Torriano Avenue
London NW5 2RZ

A Year in the Life of the Isle of Skye
Copyright © 2008 Frances Lincoln Limited

All text and photographs copyright © 2008 Bill Birkett,
except for photograph on page 96: © Bill Birkett Photo Library
Map on page 6 by Martin Bagness
Edited and designed by Jane Havell Associates

First Frances Lincoln edition 2008

Bill Birkett has asserted his moral right to be identified as Author of this
Work in accordance with the Copyright, Designs and Patents Act 1988

British Library cataloguing-in-publication data
A catalogue record for this book is available from the British Library

ISBN 978 0 7112 2644 9

Printed in Singapore

9 8 7 6 5 4 3 2 1

contents

The Isle of Skye: Introduction   6
The Isle of Skye: History   16

strathaird and
the red cuillin   24

Weather and the seasons   52

the black cuillin   54

Flora and fauna   84

trotternish   90

People and culture   120

Climbing and mountaineering   124

Index   128

Rubha Hunish

● Duntulm

Quirang ×   Staffin Bay
● Staffin
● Uig   × Kilt Rock

Trumpan   ▲ Beinn Edra
● Stein
                                        Rona

Loch Snizort

Loch Dunvegan

● Glendale

Neist Point   ● Dunvegan

The Isle
Of
Skye

Macleod's Tables ▲
Struan ●

Loch Bracadale

Idrigill Point

Waternish

Duirinish

Trotternish

× Old Man of Storr
← Storr Lochs

Applecross

● Portree

Ben ▲
Tianavaig

▲ Dun Caan

● Raasay

Loch Harport

Braes
Sconser
● ● ● ferry

Talisker Bay

Carbost ●

Minginish

Sligachan ●   ● Glamaig

Scalpay

Black Cuillin

Red Cuillin

▲ Sgurr nan
Gillean

Glen
Brittle ●

Sgurr Alasdair ▲
Bla ▲
Bheinn

Loch Ainort

Loch
Coruisk

Strathaird

▲ Beinn
na Caillich

● Broadford

Kyle of
Lochalsh ●

bridge
● Kyleakin

Sgurr na
Coinnich ▲

summer ferry

● Kylerhea

Soay

● Elgol

Loch Slapin

Sleat

Sleat

Sound of Sleat

Knoydart

over 800 metres

650-800 metres

500-650 metres

300-500 metres

0-300 metres

● Armadale

ferry to Mallaig

10 miles

16 kilometres

north

the isle of skye introduction

There is no more elemental and evocative land than the Isle of Skye, spread like a many-fingered open wing skimming across the sea between the North-West Highlands of Scotland and the remote chain of the Outer Hebrides – surely none with greater enchantment, mystery, legend, folklore and history, nor with greater diversity of geology and physical form. It is an island where union between land and sea is so intimate, so entwined, that landscapes and seascapes fuse inexorably to create an indelible impression.

Skye is a world of immense contrast – of mountains, desolate brown moor, sparkling lochs, roaring waterfalls, sea cliffs and white coral beaches among myriad islands floating atop clear blue seas. This romantic and magical land is rich in history, the backdrop to the defeated Bonnie Prince Charlie's flight from the English in 1746. Expansive, free and unencumbered, this world of big skies and sweeping vistas is an ever-changing kaleidoscope of light, mood and expression, with conditions varying from flat calm to howling gale; the wild province of eagle, deer, salmon, killer whale and seal, of rose-root and rare alpines.

Like the golden eagle which soars on the wind, from huge form to tiny pinprick in the blink of an eye, Skye seems to defy the ordinary rules of time and space. On clear days, across a great pool of silver, it appears that you can reach out and touch the distant chain of the Outer Hebrides, many miles distant. Yet when the clouds drift among the rocky heights, the near mountains look impossibly high and impenetrably distant. This is a land where weather patterns are complex and notoriously unpredictable. The Vikings, whose stronghold this was for five hundred years, knew the island as 'Ski Ey' which translates as the Cloud Island. The Celts, in Scottish Gaelic, called it 'An t-Eilean Sgitheanach', the Winged Isle; also 'Eilean a Cheo', the Isle of Mist.

There are six distinct and unique regions of hills, of striking geological diversity. The most famous is the Black Cuillin, comprised of volcanic gabbro, one of the roughest rocks in the world – a spectacular chain of naked rocky peaks linked by a long narrow ridge. It is known to mountaineers as the British Alps. Scarcely less impressive, across the long, broad valley of Glen Sligachan, are the mountains of Strathaird and the Red Cuillin, made of gabbro and the visually appealing red granite. Another key area of high hills and great sea cliffs is the long finger-peninsula of Trotternish, the most northerly tip of the Winged Isle. The rocks here are volcanic lavas, with dykes of dolerite underlain by fossil-rich sedimentary rocks and limestones. The other three areas of hills, south to north, are Sleat, Minginish and the Islands of the Inner Sound, the finger-peninsulas of Duirinish and Waternish.

In all, the Isle covers around 1,660 square kilometres, and is around 80 kilometres long by 40 across at its widest. The coastline, though difficult to measure with accuracy because of its many intricacies, is around an astonishing 725 kilometres in length. The general points of arrival and departure (for those not sailing their own boats!) are, in anti-clockwise order: Armadale on the Sound of Sleat by ferry from Mallaig; Kylerhea, a summer service only by little ferry across the narrow northern neck of the Sound of Sleat; Kyleakin by bridge from Kyle of Lochalsh on the mainland, and Uig by ferry from the Outer Hebrides. Broadford is the second largest 'town,' while Portree is the largest and regarded as the capital.

I was a child when I first heard of the Isle of Skye, via the radio and a rendition of the famous 'Skye Boat Song':

> Speed bonnie boat like a bird on the wing,
> Onward the sailors cry,
> Carry the lad that is born to be king,
> Over the sea to Skye.

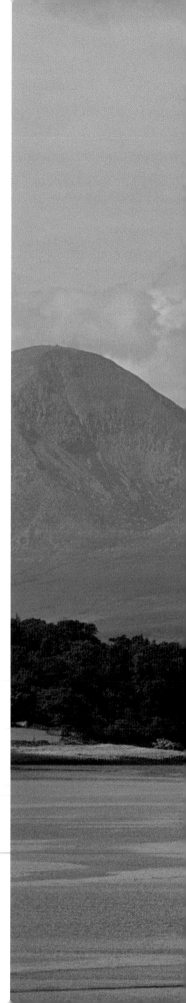

OPPOSITE: The Skye Bridge over the narrow sea inlet of Kyle Akin stretches from the island of Eilean Ban, now connected to the mainland and Kyle of Lochalsh by causeway, to a point just north of Kyleakin. Built by private enterprise, it was opened in 1995. The toll charged was always controversial and was fought by SKAT (Skye and Kyle Against Tolls); it was eventually dropped by the newly formed Scottish Parliament, which purchased the bridge in 2004. Apart from the charging of tolls, the effects of the bridge on the community of Skye have been far-reaching. To me, building a bridge seemed a step in the wrong direction, one that denigrated the independent nature of the Isle. Of course, with my civil engineer's eye, I can see that the high, long, concrete arch has a certain elegance and grandeur – it could have been a positive asset if built over the Thames! To the right is Eilean Ban, where otter man Gavin Maxwell once lived, author of the best-selling Ring of Bright Water. The hills beyond are mostly those of the Red Cuillin.

I was immediately captivated by this lyrical ballad and its vivid imagery, though I had no idea then that this was the true tale of Bonnie Prince Charlie's escape from the English, disguised as Flora MacDonald's maid, sailing back to Skye whence he had begun his ill-fated though incredibly bold campaign to return the Stuarts to the throne of Scotland and England. In fact, it was a while before I realised that Skye was a place, not the sky above the sea, and that there was something other than a metaphysical meaning to the song. Learning that Skye was indeed a land of magnificent mountains, defiance and incredible history was enthralling. When the literal meaning of the song began to dawn on me, Skye was the place I wanted to go to.

It took some time, for though we travelled to the Highlands of Scotland for our two-week family holiday every year, my father, typically, refused to take me to Skye on the premise that it always rained and time was too short. He had a point. It wasn't until a climbing friend of mine, Charlie Leventon, secured a summer job as custodian to the Glen Brittle Memorial Hut and was allowed to be accompanied by one friend, free of charge, that I got there. I stayed for virtually the whole of June 1972. Endless days of rain failed to dampen our spirits or enthusiasm: we simply climbed lightweight and kept moving, soloing as many classic routes as we could in the knowledge that, whatever we did in the Cuillin, we were in for a soaking.

On that trip I learnt two valuable things. One was that if you could get beyond Glen Brittle and the influence of the Cuillin, instead of rolling mists, lashing rain and driving wind there were tranquillity, sunshine and an astonishing quality and variety of landscape. The other was simply that I was in love with the Isle of Skye: it got under my skin. Though I spent the rest of that summer in the French and Swiss Alps, despite their challenge and grandeur I yearned to be back on Skye with my hands and feet on the gabbro rocks of the Cuillin or attempting to climb some of the vertical sea cliffs I had discovered. I returned in September as autumn slipped in. More rain, but it didn't matter a jot.

This book is a personal photographic essay portraying the Isle of Skye throughout the seasons, from its awakening in spring to the icy grip of winter. In particular it focuses on the three key areas: the Red Cuillin and Strathaird, the Black Cuillin, and the most northerly and spectacular finger of the wing, the region of Trotternish.

The tour

The most usual way to get to the island is from Kyle of Lochalsh to Kyleakin over the narrow stretch of water known as Kyle Akin. From this point the main A87 travels up the east coast to Portree before transferring to the west side of the finger peninsula of Trotternish to terminate at Uig. Splitting off below Portreee at the Sligachan Hotel, the A863 follows the west coast to Dunvegan. The A850 links Dunvegan to Portree. Within this overall framework of major roads exists a spider's web of lesser roads feeding the tiny townships and scattered communities that typify life in this remote and thinly populated land. On Skye, of course, 'major road' is a relative term – many of the lesser roads are single-track with passing places

Kyle of Lochalsh is served by rail, a fact that made the Cuillin mountains relatively accessible and therefore popular with the early pioneers of mountaineering. In 1995 a bridge replaced the ferry over Kyle Akin, even though many would have preferred the old ferry to remain. Before the bridge, Skye was unequivocally an island, and you had to be psychologically committed to a stay – it wasn't just another day trip, but felt as if you were entering a faraway and different land. Undeniably, as with any improvement in communications, the bridge has accelerated the removal of the old and assisted

development of the new. Life now moves at a quicker pace and dances to a different, less traditional, tune.

Before you reach the great arch of the concrete bridge, a peninsula now leads to and over the once separate island of Eilean Ban. This was home to Gavin Maxwell, author of the 1960s masterpiece *Ring of Bright Water*. For someone so responsible for the reawakening of the general public to the wonders and philosophy of the natural world, particularly that of the otter, Maxwell led an extraordinary and contradictory life, including the founding of a shark station on Soay, an island just south of the Cuillin, from which he hunted and harpooned the harmless basking shark!

Over the water, south of Kyleakin, stand the remains of the circular tower of Caisteal Maol, said to be the fabled stronghold of a Norse princess who once controlled these waters. Another, or perhaps the same, princess is reputedly buried beneath a huge cairn on the summit of the Red Cuillin mountain Beinn na Caillich above Broadford. As with the whole of Skye, myth and legend are inexorably entwined here – it is quite probable that the cairn atop Beinn na Caillich dates from prehistory while the existing castle remains are medieval.

Once landed at Kyleakin, the natural migration is north-wards towards the pleasant town of Broadford and an intersection of ways. Before Broadford a road leads off south down Glen Arroch, between the heights of Sleat – Sgurr na Coinnich to the north and Ben Aslak to the south – to the car ferry of Glenelg (summer only). The mainland approach to this ferry from Shiel Bridge gives breathtaking views back to the Five Sisters of Kintail.

Once at Broadford, the Red Cuillin lies ahead and behind can be found Sleat and the southern hills of Skye. Following the road south leads to Armadale and the Sound of Sleat, where the ferry lands from Mallaig. Relatively sheltered and fertile, this is the most luxuriant and tree-covered area of Skye. Clan Donald

has a Visitor Centre by Armadale Castle and there are cultivated gardens to visit. Nearby is Sabhal Mor Ostaig, the University of Gaelic.

West from Broadford the narrow road to the hamlet of Elgol follows a route flanking the southern boundary of the Red Cuillin and Strathaird mountains. Initially it travels through the fascinating valley of Strath Suardal. The limestone of Ben Suardal with its rich mountain flora stands to the south and Beinn na Caillich to the north. The ruins of Cill Chriosad church, the abandoned buildings and railway of the old marble works and the reeds of Loch Cill Chriosad catch the eye. However, unseen, over the hills to the south, lie the ruined villages of Boreag and Suisinish, victims of the Clearances:

> Burned are our homes, exile and death
> Scatter the loyal men,
> Yet e'er the sword cool in the sheath
> Charlie will come again.

As the road runs through Torrin, one of the finest mountain views in the whole of Skye looks over Loch Slapin to the mighty face of Bla Bheinn. The scene is enhanced by the intrusion of white marble beneath the waters of the loch, which often gives it the colour of translucent aquamarine, contrasting wonder-fully with the stark black gabbro soaring high above. Contin-uing along the opposite side of the loch, the road passes through Glasnakille and over the celebrated Spar Cave (hidden from view) before going down to the hamlet of Elgol. From the shores of Loch Scavaig, by Elgol's old school house and the jetty, there is a tremendous aspect over the Cuillin mountains. A short coastal walk to the south, over sandstone cliffs and inlets, leads to one of the numerous Prince Charlie's caves.

At the time of writing, two boat operators run a regular spring and summer service over Loch Scavaig from Elgol to a landing pier beneath the falls of Scavaig and Loch Coruisk.

Loch Coruisk, inaccessible and remote, lies at the very heart of the Black Cuillin mountains – it is one of the most evocative wild places in Britain. Walter Scott visited it in 1814 and the following year published 'The Lord of the Isles':

> For rarely human eye has known
> A scene so stern as that dread lake
> With its dark ledge of barren stone

Turner painted it to illustrate Scott's poems in 1831.

Heading north from Broadford, the road flanks the western edge of the Red Cuillin by the shores of Loch Ainort, before passing beneath Glamaig to Sconser with views out to the Isle of Raasay and its distinctive cone of Dun Caan, the volcano mountain. A regular ferry from Sconser to Raasay carries cars and is relatively inexpensive. The road meets the inlet of Loch Sligachan, leading to the Sligachan Hotel and again a parting of the ways. The hotel, a popular base for mountaineering in the Cuillin since the 1880s, remains justifiably popular, with a recent extension, facilitation of a micro-brewery and a camp-site. Beyond, an unforgettable landscape is forged by one of the most magnificent mountain skylines: the northern end of the great Cuillin Ridge, the peak of Sgurr nan Gillean with Am Basteir (the Executioner) and the Bhasteir Tooth (the Executioner's Axe) to its right.

The valley of Glen Sligachan (path only), leading south from the opposite bank of the river to the hotel, forms the boundary between the Red Cuillin and Strathaird to the east and the Black Cuillin to the west. North, the road leads directly to Portree, while the fork to the left opens up the western edge of the Cuillin, defined by Glen Brittle, and Minginish.

Of the numerous routes off the main west coast road to Dunvegan the most travelled is that leading to Carbost and either down to Glen Brittle or on to Talisker, home of the famous Skye whisky distillery, and further still the magnificent Talisker Bay. Glen Brittle gives access to many highlights of the Cuillin massif, including the great cliffs of Sron na Ciche, Sgurr Alasdair (the highest peak in the Cuillin at 993m) and Sgurr Dearg's much photographed Inaccessible Pinnacle. Facilities include a popular campsite, a youth hostel, a mountaineering hut, scattered bed and breakfast accommodation and little else. Long may it remain so.

Heading north along the main road in the direction of Dunvegan provides a great view back to the distant Black Cuillin over Loch Harport. By Bracadale, a minor road climbs to provide a direct link with Portree on the opposite side of the island, before the main road continues through the village of Struan. To the west, Ardtrek and its lonely lighthouse provide a wistful foreground to the huge sea cliffs of Rubha nan Clach

ABOVE: A peep along the jagged peaks of the Black Cuillin ridge, looking north over Coire Lagan, from the top of the great climber's cliff of Sron na Ciche. The Black Cuillin are famed among mountaineers and known as 'the British Alps'; a full traverse of the ridge is recognised as the finest mountaineering expedition in Britain. The highest point seen here is the Inaccessible Pinnacle, whose top rises to 986m from the summit crest of Sgurr Dearg. The mighty, sharp-topped peaks of Sgurr a' Ghreadaidh and Sgurr a' Mhadaidh lie beyond.

LEFT: Shinty is the traditional game of the Western Isles and Highlands. It is fast, furious and amazingly skilful, with players using stick, hands and feet to control a ball often propelled at lightning speed. The weather was so wet during this particular match at Portree that the game had to be abandoned. That's really wet!

beyond. At low tide it is possible to walk out to the island of Oronsay from Ullinish Point, but I would recommend a careful check of the tide tables, allowing plenty of time, before you do. Nearby, Dun Beag stands just above the road.

After this point, Loch Bracadale opens to the left. Beyond its numerous islands it is possible to make out the distant silhouette of Macleod's Maidens, the sea stacks off Idrigill Point. A little further along the sea loch, the flat-topped mountains of Healabhal Bheag and Healabhal Mhor, Macleod's Tables, add drama to an already powerful scene of sea and sky. Soon Dunvegan is reached, with campsites and plentiful accommodation. The word 'town' is perhaps too extravagant a description – it is more like an extended village, but with shops and garage facilities. Dunvegan Castle and gardens, stronghold of the MacLeods for some eight hundred years, is open to the public. The Coral Beaches lie at the end of the road leading north past the castle and provide a short and rewarding walk.

West of Dunvegan, the most westerly finger of the Winged Isle is known as Duirinish. The road leads first by MacLeod's Tables and then by Glendale, the township and home of the Glendale Martyrs who were instrumental in standing against the Clearances in the late nineteenth century and shaming the British Government into setting up a Royal Commission to investigate the distressed condition of the Highlanders. The western terminus of the road lies above the dramatic peninsula of Neist Point, its lighthouse and buildings surrounded by vertical cliffs. The sea and a distant outline of the Outer Hebrides lie to the west. The peninsula north and slightly east of Dunvegan is Waternish. The road leads past Stein, a lovely harbour with reputedly the oldest inn on Skye, to the ruined church of Trumpan, scene of yet another clan massacre, near the end of the road.

Jumping back to the east coast we have the sheltered harbour and town of Portree, the 'capital' of Skye, with its fine

hotels, inns, restaurants and cafés, bakery, shops and the studio of the artist Tommy MacKenzie. To those who have camped in the wilder reaches of the island, this feels like every facility known to man! Portree hosts the annual Skye Games, with assorted events including piping, dancing, and field and track athletics with a difference. In 1990 the shinty team, under the management of my great friend Ross Cowie, won the coverted Camanachd Cup, the equivalent of winning the Premiership League in English football. Boat trips run from the harbour and it's a great, buzzing place to be.

Back in 1972 I suffered a puncture in my motorbike tyre and ordered a replacement inner tube at the main garage in Portree. Every few days I would walk and hitch-hike from Glen Brittle to the garage, to be reassured by the same response – for sure, the new tube would arrive from Fort William tomorrow. After two weeks' waiting, I saw a motorbike chugging through the main street of Portree. On instinct, adopting the 'bikers unite in an emergency' code, I chased after it – it was a Velocette 500, carrying a pillion passenger and a cat in a basket! – and managed to catch up, jump in front of it and stop it. Had they a spare inner tube that would fit my bike? Of course, who would travel the remoter regions of the Scottish Highlands without one? Could I buy it from them? No! But I could have it for nothing. Portree has always been a special sort of place.

The final road north leads around Trotternish, the most northerly, wildest and apparently most desolate of all Skye's peninsulas. Here lie many sights and experiences that make the Isle of Skye that special place on the edge of existence. The great craggy face of Storr stands above the pear-shaped 55m pinnacle of the Old Man of Storr, with the Storr Lochs below. These rocks are a particularly crumbly type of volcanic lava spewed from an ancient volcano: the late, great Don Whillans climbed the Old Man in 1955, followed soon after by Patsy Walsh, but the ascent has scarcely been repeated since.

OPPOSITE: Looking to the distinctive flat-topped mountains known as Macleod's Tables, a spectacular view north-west over Loch Bracadale from just above the little settlement of Ullinish. Healabhal Bheag (South Table), 489m, lies to the left and the lower Healabhal Mhor (North Table) to the right. These celebrated heights in Duirinish, the most westerly peninsula of Skye, can be ascended by making a horseshoe traverse of about 11km, starting from the road just north of Orbost. Stories tell that the Ninth Chief of the MacLeods invited lowland chiefs from the King's Court in Edinburgh, with the promise that he had a grander banqueting hall with a roof more lofty and a table more ample than anything to be found in the King's Palace. Sure enough, they had to admit that the torch-lit top of Healabhal Mhor was indeed such a place! Legend also tells of a supernatural force levelling the tops to provide bed and table for St Columba; geologists, however, claim that the flat tops are due to the erosion of horizontally stratified basalt lavas.

Beyond this the road begins to hug the coastline, which sports impressive cliffs and open views across the Sound of Raasay over the isles of Raasay and Rona to the Torridon and Applecross mountains of the Scottish mainland. A viewpoint by Loch Mealt, situated above the 55m free-falling Waterfall of Mealt, reveals the folded pleats of the stunning verticality of Kilt Rock. A challenging place to rock climb outside the Cuillin, it was first climbed in the 1980s when Ed Grindley and others, including myself, made a number of first ascents. Strong winds can blow here. On numerous occasions I have seen the fall of the water reversed to blow back over the top of the cliff, soaking the innocent and unsuspecting on the viewing platform.

We used to camp in the picnic area. Once a coachload of Australian tourists arrived as I was brewing up tea. One came back from the rails guarding the cliff edge to urge me look, with the words 'killer whale'. I carefully explained to him that it was a basking shark. Not for the first time, I was completely wrong. A huge black-and-white beast was rising and falling through the waves, undoubtedly a killer whale. We were all jumping with excitement at the unexpected and unbelievable sight.

Beyond the Kilt Rock at Ellishader, a visit to local expert Dugald Ross's Staffin Museum is worthwhile. Flint arrowheads, flintlock rifles and spectacular fossils from the sedimentary rocks underlying the volcanics – not only did he find and identify all the exhibits himself, he actually built the museum with his own hands. Its most famous holdings are dinosaur fossils, including the leg bone of a large sauropod (a long-necked, Brontosaurus-type of dinosaur) and the ulna and radius of a thyreophoran dinosaur (an armoured dinosaur, possibly a Stegosaurus).

On to Staffin and its beautiful bay. Turn left here if you want to climb the amazing Staffin–Uig Pass which winds its way up an impossibly steep hillside. Just north, poised on the slopes of Meall na Suiramach above Staffin, is the great landslip of the Quirang, with its weird pinnacles surrounding the serene golf-course-like feature known as the Table. Further on, Flodigarry boasts a fine hotel and exotic bar (its walls are decorated with the writings of the Koran!). A cottage in the grounds is the one-time home of the heroine Flora MacDonald, who smuggled Bonnie Prince Charlie from South Uist in the Outer Hebrides to Skye on a wild night in 1746:

> Loud the winds howl, loud the winds roar,
> Thunderclaps rend the air,
> Baffled, our foes stand on the shore,
> Follow they will not dare.
>
> Through the waves' leap, soft shall ye sleep,
> Ocean's a royal bed,
> Rocked in the deep, Flora will keep
> Watch by your weary head.

LEFT: A thatched 'blackhouse' croft, now part of The Skye Museum of Island Life at Kilmuir on the east coast of north Trotternish. Flora MacDonald's monument lies just above the museum.

BELOW: The remote telephone box at Duntulm is the best starting point for a walk to the wonderful headland of Rubha Hunish. Here, Dave Birkett carries the 60m rope which we used in an ascent of the extremely difficult Sailing Too Far From Shore in September 1996, at the time the hardest rock climb on the Isle.

Duntulm, the most northerly outpost, has a hotel, a castle, a ruined crofting village and a vague path which leads out to the magnificent headland of Rubha Hunish, one of the wildest and most intriguing localities imaginable, with uninterrupted views to the Shiant Isles, in the shape of a school of whales, and the Isle of Lewis beyond. The great horseshoe of cliffs here are most spectacular and have provided me with many an adventure. The last bow-shaped tent of the travelling people that I ever saw in Scotland was erected near the roadside here. Once I watched sweeping searchlights of green beams, the Northern Lights, play across the Outer Hebrides for hours.

A folk museum at Clachan on the road to Uig on the west coast utilises old thatched 'blackhouses' that once dotted the region. Many years ago, my wife bought me a pullover here, made from the wool of a Scottish Blackface sheep. Two decades and much use later, it is still my favourite item of 'high-tech' clothing! Nearby, above the road at Kilmuir, stands the memorial to the courageous Flora MacDonald who was carted off to imprisonment in the Tower of London for her rescue of Charlie after his defeat at the Battle of Culloden. The epitaph on the memorial, written by Dr Johnson, reads: 'A name that will be mentioned in history, and if courage and fidelity be virtues, mentioned with honour.'

Many's the lad fought on the day,
Well the claymore did wield,

When the night came, silently lay
Dead on Culloden's field.

A short run now to Uig – and how incongruous, after so much wilderness and wildness, to see the great red, black and white Caledonian MacBrayne ferry, 'Lord of The Isles', steaming into port from Lochmaddy in the Western Isles. There are a couple of inns here and the Isle of Skye Brewery which produces some fine real ales, notably the aptly named Am Basteir (the Executioner).

The road back to Portree leads by the side of Loch Snizort with amazing and ever-changing light and views over the Ascrib Islands to Waternish. Just about the full range of Skye's prehistory, in the form of standing stones, hut circles, duns, brochs and chambered cairns, can be viewed from the road for those with the patience to observe. For me, one of the most interesting of these relics is the intricately carved Pictish Symbol Stone, which stands beside the road in Tote – one of only three ever found in the whole of Scotland. I don't know what it represents and I doubt, as one of my climbing friends asked jokingly when I showed it to him, that it can predict the weather! Nevertheless, to me, inanimate as it may seem, it is an object of considerable power. And I really don't care what the weather does on the incomparable Isle of Skye – just to be there is all that really matters.

the isle of skye history

Prehistory

I find it both exciting and surprising to realise that man came to Skye within so short a time after the last Ice Age. Latest research puts the final retreat of the ice cap at c. 8000 BC; Mesolithic hunter-gatherers, who began following herds of animals migrating from Europe, arrived within a thousand years. Evidence of these early Stone Age peoples has been found just above the narrow road down to Staffin Slip in Trotternish – the first such site to be found on Skye and one of only a handful discovered in Scotland. A camp and midden pile of shells, dated c. 6500 BC, reveals that these early visitors also had a taste for seafood in addition to meat. Incidentally, despite the obvious importance of the site, when the road down to the jetty was widened in the early 1990s the way was blasted after covering the site merely with protective sheeting. It now rests below a pile of rock rubble!

Evidence of prehistory litters the landscape of Skye. With little development in terms of settlement, industry and modern agriculture, much of the landscape has been left undisturbed for millennia. Most visible, scattered liberally over the landscape, are the duns and brochs, defensive sites accredited to the Iron Age.

Although perhaps not so spectacular or easily recognised, there is much further evidence of man's impact on the landscape. Having roamed over many different and remote parts of the Isle with an interested and one-time land surveyor's/civil engineer's eye, I have noticed a considerable number of man-made features which I suspect are prehistoric. Hardly any are documented, and of those only a small fraction have been investigated or interpreted.

Around all the coastal areas I have walked and climbed there are extensive earthworks, burial mounds and field systems, often a complex mixture ranging from ruined crofting townships of relatively recent origin, to burial mounds, earth-

works and stone structures from the Neolithic (c. 4500–2,000 BC), Bronze Age (c. 2000–500 BC) and Iron Age (c. 500 BC–400 AD). Among the hills, in the high valleys, following many watercourses and burns, particularly between the confluences, are a multitude of earth and stone burial mounds. Why they follow these watercourses so enthusiastically I'm not qualified to say, though it may be due to a belief that running water bears the spirit of the dead to the afterlife. This practice was followed even in Christian times, with Skye's remarkable 'Cathedral to the Isles', dating from the early eleventh century, found on Skeabost Island in the River Snizort, just off the Portree–Dunvegan road, above the head of Loch Snizort.

A brief rundown on what is officially recognised on Skye is as follows. Mesolithic hunter-gatherers used stone tools made in Scotland – from pitchstone found on the Isle of Arran, a remarkable glass-like material that looks as if it has been scattered like a meteor shower over the granite hills of that island, and bloodstone from the Isle of Rum. These peoples also used dug-out canoes and travelled by sea. To migrate from Europe and survive at the recolonisation of flora and fauna following the last Ice Age, they were clearly extremely proficient.

The Neolithic period began on Skye around 5000 BC when these peoples began farming domestic animals and cultivating crops. Perhaps some of the ancient field systems around the coast and the protective earth banks on the edges of the cliffs come from this early period. Chambered cairns (stone burial tombs), notably Rubh an Dunain at the tip of Loch Brittle's southern peninsula (an interesting walk from the campsite), are certainly identified from this period, as are the flint arrowheads found with these tombs.

Evidence in the form of distinguished pots show that the Beaker People, skilled in metal manufacture and craftsmanship, were on Skye around 2000 BC. This period, the beginning of the Bronze Age, could be classed as the first to bring the Celtic

OPPOSITE: Dun Beag, thought to be Iron Age in origin, is one of the best-preserved brochs on the Isle. It stands in a commanding position above Struanmore, just a couple of minutes' walk from the west coast road below Dunvegan. The full significance of these spiral stone turrets, prevalent throughout the Western Isles and Highlands, remains the subject of debate. Some say they were purely defensive, built to protect coastal communities from attack by sea. Others suggest that their intricate internal structure was designed to radiate heat effectively from centrally located fires, protecting people from extremes of rain and wind.

FAR LEFT: This ancient gravestone outside the ruins of Trumpan Church on the Waternish peninsula bears an inscription which might be Viking. The church was reputedly the scene of an infamous clan massacre, when a party of MacDonalds from Uist landed at Ardmore Bay one Sunday in May 1578 and set fire to it, killing the entire MacLeod congregation except for one girl. She raised the alarm, and the retreating MacDonalds were duly slaughtered in turn.

LEFT: The Clach Ard monolith of hard dolerite rock stands in the little community of Tote, between Portreee and Dunvegan. A Pictish Symbol Stone, it displays a complex pattern of circles, spirals and ellipses.

tradition and language to the island. The Beaker People originated from the Rhine Valley and are thought to have constructed hill forts of both timber and stone, notably Dun Skudiburgh and Dun Gerashader.

The Iron Age is particularly noted for impressive cone-like stone structures known as brochs, of which there are around twenty recognised sites on Skye alone. Precisely built from large blocks of stone, their purpose and period is still a little hazy. They are thought to be defensive: a community, or the leaders of a community, could seek safety and shelter from invasion, such as a raid from the sea. Within the thick stone walls of the broch, to which access could be effectively blocked off, spiral passages and staircases could accommodate those seeking protection. Dun Beag above Struan is the best known; two further impressive examples stand on the mainland at Gleann Beag, near the Glenelg Ferry.

The culture of this era, extending into Roman times, appears as yet to be little understood. Roman writers in around 300 AD called the tribes of people living north of Antonine's Wall *Pictae* – the Picts or 'painted people'. Antonine's Wall was a Roman defensive fortification between the Forth and Clyde in central Scotland, built in honour of Emperor Antoninus Pius by Lollius Urbicus, Governor of Britain, in around 143 AD. It established a frontier to the north of Hadrian's Wall in England, with the intention of restraining the Pictish tribes to the north; as such it represents the north-western boundary of the Roman Empire. However, residual hostile tribes in the southern uplands of Scotland forced more than one retreat down to the safety of Hadrian's Wall, and the Antonine Wall was probably completely abandoned by 180 AD. Some time within this period (the dating of all this seems to me to be somewhat confused), the Pictish Symbol Stone at Tote must have been carved and, supposedly, though they may well come from a much earlier period, the intriguing underground structures

known as souterrains were built. There are numerous examples of these on Skye – one of the best preserved lies above the Allt na Cille around 1km north of Glasnakille near Elgol.

Post-Christianity

The last two thousand years are hardly less confusing. When, in the later stages, the complications of religion, crown and state are added it is a very difficult picture to interpret. For example, when a contingent of Skye men marched from the island to, as they thought, support Bonnie Prince Charlie at Culloden, they found on arrival that their clan chief commanded them to fight on the side of the English and the Duke of Cumberland! At Culloden more Scots fought against Bonnie Prince Charlie and his Jacobite cause than for them.

Celts, known as Scots (from whom the name Scotland came, despite the fact that the first Celts arrived much earlier and where known as Picts), migrated to Skye and the Scottish west coast from Ireland around 500 AD. They imported the modern Gaelic language, the skill of writing, and Christianity in the form of St Columba who visited in 585 AD. Many island names come from this date, though it is important to realise that Gaelic did not have an exclusive influence on the language and nomenclature of Skye.

The order rapidly changed again with Viking raids which began around 800 AD. Hungry for land, the Norse soon settled and Skye became a Viking stronghold for something like five hundred years. Many Skye names are of direct Norse origin – indeed, perhaps many of the present-day crofting villages and townships, and those ruined due to the Clearances, were originally built by the Norse, typically Fiskavaig and Ullinish. The names Waternish, Duirinish, Trotternish and Minginish are all Norse in origin. So are many mountain names, such as Healabhal (MacLeod's Tables) and Storr. The most famous of them all, Cuillin, comes from the Norse *kiolen*, meaning high ridge,

ABOVE: A carved stone relief on a burial slab in the Mortuary Chapel on St Columba's Island, said to hold the graves of 28 Nicholson clan chiefs. The island, on the River Snizort at the head of Loch Snizort near Skeabost, was the site of the cathedral church of the Bishops of the Isles from 1079 to 1498.

from its likeness to the upturned keel of a boat. Of course, many names are now a mixture of the different influences.

Norse rule came to an end with the defeat of King Haakon in 1263. By the time the Lord of The Isles came to hold sway, a position assumed by the Chief of Clan Donald in 1354, a clan system had developed in Skye that regarded itself as separate from mainland Scotland. Despite this sense of independence, when King James IV of Scotland abolished the Lordship of The Isles in 1493, the clans of Skye, notably the MacLeods and the MacDonalds, entered the ensuing free-for-all age of plunder with gusto. Massacre followed massacre as reprisal and revenge became the order of the day – until the final battle of 1601 after which James VI of Scotland interceded to calm the situation down.

On the death of Elizabeth I of England in 1603, James VI of Scotland also became James 1 of England, uniting the two countries. In 1609 James VI and 1 took things a stage further in an attempt to control the clans of the Western Isles. He summoned the Hebridean Chiefs to Iona and forced them to sign up to the Statutes of Icolmkill (the Gaelic name for Iona). Nine statutes, calling for the improvement and order of the Isles as defined by the King, were seen as an attempt to end the traditional Gaelic way of life. Naturally, this was not to the liking of the clans; possibly the most unpleasant slap in the face was the banning of *uisgebeatha* (water of life or *aqua vitae*), pronounced in English as whisky.

Inclusive of the Western Isles, this was an age of intense religious debate and radical politics. In England, both contributed to a bloody civil war in the 1600s between Crown and Parliament (the Cavaliers and the Roundheads), resulting in a parliamentary victory for Oliver Cromwell and the dramatic execution of the then Stuart King, Charles I. A short-lived republic was followed by the Restoration of the Crown in 1660, by which Charles II was made king. He was succeeded in 1685 by his brother King James VII of Scotland and II of England. James did not last long, and fled to France in 1688 after the Glorious Revolution.

The Glorious Revolution was brought on by disenchantment with the Catholic Stuarts. Parliament and influential merchants wanted stability and prosperity, and sought it under the Dutch William of Orange. Nominally, William invaded Britain to take over the reins of power, but in truth it was a bloodless coup; he was persuaded to come. He married Mary Stuart and the couple ascended the throne as joint monarchs (a first) and defenders of Protestantism. The Act of Settlement in 1701 effectively ensured that only Protestants could reign.

On the death first of Mary and then of William, Mary's sister Anne was crowned Queen of England and Scotland in 1702. When the Stuart dynasty ended with the death of the Protestant Queen Anne, it had reigned over England and Scotland from 1603 to 1714. This was a period which saw a flourishing court culture but very little for the common man or Western Islander to be thrilled about. It was a time of much upheaval and instability, of plague, fire and war. The Stuart legacy was to linger on for another century in the form of claimants to the throne, but many in Scotland and England felt that the dynasty had passed its sell-by date, whatever its rights of ascendancy by blood line.

Following the Treaty of Union between Scotland and England in 1707, the German House of Hanover succeeded and King George I of Great Britain was crowned in 1714 – it is said that he did not speak a single word of English or Gaelic! Varous Jacobite uprisings came to nothing, yet Stuart princes remained in the wings. When Bonnie Prince Charlie, Charles Edward Stuart or the Young Pretender (grandson of the Catholic King James VII and II) landed on Eriskay, a small island in the Outer Hebrides, he was allegedly told to go home (i.e. to France). He retorted, 'I am come home, sir,' despite the fact that he was setting foot on British soil for the first time. I suppose at least he could speak English, if not Gaelic! Charles was determined, against all odds, to drive George II from the British throne and establish his father as King James VIII and III. Whatever rights he may or may not have had, the clan leaders of Skye, notably the MacDonalds and MacLeods, saw his campaign as dangerous and ill-founded, with little or no benefit for the Western Islanders. Perhaps the banning of the whisky still loomed large in their memory of Stuart power!

Nevertheless, Charlie pressed on, and support from the mainland clans grew to some 6,000 strong. Possibly with the promise of French troops, arms and supplies, he managed to march his highland army south to Derby undefeated. He was within striking distance of London when it became obvious to his advisors and commander Lord George Murray that no further help was forthcoming. As it was, King George II had already packed his bags and hailed a cab; Charlie could have walked into London virtually unopposed! To have got so far, from an indifferent and faltering start in the remote Highlands, is proof of the extraordinary bravery and tenacity of his men. Whether he could have held London, against the approaching armies of the Duke of Cumberland and General Wade, we shall never know.

Charlie followed advice to retreat and got as far as Inverness and Culloden. Dispirited and exhausted, in April 1746 his Highland army made their last stand. It was a bad day for the Highlanders; outgunned and outmanned, they were heavily defeated. What followed earned the Duke of Cumberland, son of George II, the nickname 'the Butcher'. The atrocities did not end at the battlefield; reprisals and the effective break-up of the Highland clan system followed.

The escape of Charlie and his eventual safe return to the French court has become the stuff of legend, much celebrated in song. During the five months of his flight across the Western Highlands and Isles, despite a reward of £30,000, an absolute

fortune in those times, not a single Highlander betrayed him. To me that says a lot about the courage, integrity and compassion of the Western Highlanders and Islanders.

The most celebrated was undoubtedly the plucky Flora MacDonald who sailed him over from Benbecula to Kilbride in Trotternish on Skye, disguised as her serving woman, Betty Burke. Intriguingly, her stepfather, Hugh MacDonald, was in charge of the local militia controlling the island on behalf of George II and the Hanoverian government, and it was he who aquired the appropriate papers for her to cross the heavily guarded Little Minch.

Was Charlie a fool with grandiose ideas or an extremely brave and valiant man? Perhaps he was both. The bottom line of his campaign, however, was that many people lay dead, and the lives of ordinary Western Islanders became markedly worse following his intervention.

On a lighter note, and probably of greater consequence in introducing the Isle of Skye to the wider world, Dr Samuel Johnson travelled with James Boswell to the Western Isles in 1773 in a trip that could be regarded as the beginning of tourism. A young and enthusiastic Boswell had befriended Johnson in London in ten years earlier. Johnson was England's most famous man of letters, with an affinity for Scotland; he produced the first English dictionary in 1755, and is famed for his many pithy sayings (for example, 'A fishing rod is a stick with a *hook* at one end and a *fool* at the other'). Boswell was a Scotch advocate and produced one of the most celebrated biographies ever written in the English language, *The Life of Samuel Johnson LL.D.* Johnson's enthusiasm for Scotland had initially been fired by the works of Martin Martin (Mhartainn MacGill Mhartainn), a Gaelic speaker who came from Bealach near Duntulm at the northern tip of Trotternish, who had published *A Description of the Western Isles of Scotland* in 1703. The two men went to Scotland in the late summer and

autumn of 1773, only 23 years after the flight of the Bonnie Prince, riding north from Edinburgh to Inverness and then westward through the Great Glen and across the mountains to the coast. Both wrote accounts of the journey, important social-history documents of the Highlands in the period following Culloden. They did much to tell Flora MacDonald's courageous story, and the epitaph on her memorial gravestone is taken from the writings of Dr Johnson.

As has always been the case in modern history, the men from Skye, despite all, have rallied to the call of the British nation in times of war. The Napoleonic War of 1806–14 was no exception. Some 7,000 men marched from Skye, a massive figure considering that today's entire population only numbers around 9,000 inhabitants. Then, however, the population of Skye was around 23,000, having doubled between 1755 and 1831 despite significant emigration to the New World. It has been claimed that this was due to the introduction of inoculations against smallpox in the 1760s.

The period following the return of the surviving Skye men from war, far from being glorious in proportion to their defeat of Napoleon at Waterloo, heralded one of the blackest periods of Western Isles and Highlands history. It was the beginning of the infamous Highland Clearances. The economy of the Western Isles took a severe downturn. Crofts foundered, landlords increased rents, and evicted people from the most productive and fertile areas to introduce an economy based on sheep. What started as voluntary emigration to the New World soon became a necessity; then, as things worsened, it was brutally enforced.

In this tragic and terrible story, no acceptable excuse has ever been offered for the oppression shown to the common folk of Skye and the Highlands. In 1852 two whole communites were forcibly cleared from Suisinish and Boreag, and their dwellings burnt to the ground. On Skye alone some 3,500 people were dispossessed and forced from the land. This heart-breaking contemporary account comes from an exile on a ship bound for Australia:

> The Collen [Cuillin] mountains were in sight for several hours of passage; but when we rounded Ardnamurchan Point, the emigrants saw the sun for the last time glitter upon their splintered peaks, and one prolonged and dismal wail rose from all the parts of the vessel: the fathers and mothers held up their infant children to take a last view of the mountains of their Fatherland which in a few minutes faded from their view forever.

ABOVE: The ruined Suardal Church, Cill Chriosad, stands by the road in Strath Suardal between Broadford and Elgol in the Strathaird region of the Isle. All members of the nearby community of Boreag were forcibly cleared from their crofts and their township burnt during one of the worst chapters of the notorious nineteenth-century Highland Clearances.

Towards the end of the century resistance eventually began to grow among the law-abiding Islanders. On Lord Mac-Donald's estate at Braes near Portree, a 16-year-old grievance with the landlord was revived: crofters demanded that grazings on Ben Lee, which had been taken over by the landlord's sheep, should be handed back to them. They refused to pay any rent for their crofts until their demands were met. Eventually, on 7 April 1882, a Sheriff's officer was sent out with summonses of ejection, to be met by a band of crofters who forced him to burn his papers. Next, fifty policemen were sent before dawn; such was the hour that confusion reigned and the men of the village were of a mind to give in. Not so the women. They had had enough and refused to give up their homes. After some pushing and shoving they began to fight back, stones were thrown and dislodged a few helmets, sticks were wielded and the children joined in. The psychological bubble had burst – the men returned to finish the job. Although a few arrests had been made, the constables left in disarray. This incident, which became known as the Battle of the Braes, was the turning point which marked the beginning of the end of the Clearances.

It was followed in quick succession by another rebellion at Glendale. After defying an interdict, three ringleaders –

including John Macpherson, the 'Glendale Martyr' – were arrested, but only with the assistance of the Marines and a gunboat called, appropriately, the *Jackal*. After trial in the Court of Session at Edinburgh, the crofters were imprisoned for two months. This aroused great public concern, and soon 21 Scottish MPs of both parties promoted a petition asking the Home Secretary to set up a Royal Commission on Highland distress. The Government gave way, and within a short time a Royal Commission was set up under Lord Napier. The result was a formidable indictment of the Highland land-owning class, and the drafting of new land laws to protect the crofter.

> Beyond the lochs of the blood of the children of men,
> beyond the frailty of the plain and the labour of the
>   mountain,
> beyond poverty, consumption, fever, agony,
> beyond hardship, wrong, tyranny, distress,
> beyond misery, despair, hatred, treachery,
> beyond guilt and defilement: watchful,
> heroic, the Cuillin is seen
> rising on the other side of sorrow.
>
> Sorley MacLean, 'The Cuillin'

ABOVE: Glendale and Loch Pooltiel, Duirinish, an area famous for the stand of the few against the many. The Glendale Martyrs defied their absent landlords and refused to be moved from their crofts. A handful of Skye men against the law, the government, the constabulary and the Marines – and they won. Their stand led to the reform of the land laws and helped bring an end to one of the most shameful periods of recent British history.

OPPOSITE: A group of shags at the entrance to Portree Harbour.

strathaird and the red cuillin

Wonderful scenery and great diversity characterise this tremendous region which offers mountains both black and red. Interest ranges from limestone caves, notably the celebrated Spar Cave, through the curvature and aestheticism of the granite Red Hills, to the powerful heights and malevolent bulk of Bla Bheinn (928m). For many, the mountain aspect of Bla Bheinn and Clach Glas, as seen over Loch Slapin, is the most impressive on the whole of Skye.

The area of Straithard and Red Cuillin is enclosed along its northern top by the main east coast, and defined along its southern tip by the west coast. It can be considered roughly triangular in shape. The top of the triangle is formed by the coastline between the Sligachan Hotel and the town of Broadford, with its inlets of Loch Sligachan and Loch Ainort. The western edge is shaped by the wide Glen Sligachan and the adjoining Strath na Creitheach. Both glens meet at the lochs of Lochan Dubha to form one long valley, which runs to the isolated white crofts at Camasunary by the shore of Loch Scavaig. This valley separates the Red from the Black Cuillin.

Beyond, as the hills decline, the peninsula runs to a point just past Elgol to form the southernmost tip of the region. The third side of the triangle is completed by the run of the Elgol–Broadford road (B8083), although in practice the western shore of Loch Slapin, beyond the road, forms the physical boundary of the area.

Principally this is a place of mountains cut through by high, desolate valleys. The southernmost hills, those of Gars-bheinn, Clach Glas and Bla Bheinn, are made of gabbro, the same as the Black Cuillin. The other hills, and there are five further groups of mountains, are comprised of red granite, giving the area its distinctive character.

The great plutonic mass of the Cuillin rose from the depths of the earth's crust in the Tertiary Period around 60 million years ago. Greenland began to float away from Europe to create the North Atlantic Ocean, resulting in volcanic action and outpourings of lava. Additionally, rifts opened in the crust and spewed out further flows of molten material.

Beneath these lavas a large chamber of magma began to cool more slowly and this resulted in the coarse crystalline gabbro of the Black Cuillin. Later, the basic magma was replaced by acid magma which broke through to form the finer-grained red granites of the Red Cuillin which sit on top of the gabbro. Erosion and glaciation have produced the dramatic forms we see now. The more jagged and angular shapes of the resistant gabbro of the Black Cuillin contrast with the softer curvature of the red granite of the Red Cuillin. The granite weathers in a more uniform manner, producing smooth outlines and fewer steep cliffs.

Around the west shore of Loch Slapin and the tip of the Strathaird peninsula around and below Elgol, the rocks are sedimentary rocks of the Jurassic Period, around 180 million years old. These are chiefly sandstones which have weathered to take on a honeycomb appearance in places. The Spar Cave at Glasnakille was produced when a basalt dyke, extruded into the sandstone, wore away more quickly than the surrounding rocks, leaving a long narrow fissure and a cave. Subsequently, calcium carbonate, leached from the limey sandstone, was deposited in the form of stalagmites. (Those visiting the cave should note that it is only accessible at low tide.)

At the geological junction of the red granite intrusion and the surrounding limestone the latter has been metamorphosed. The intense heat of the granite melted the limestone which, when cooled, turned to a beautiful marble. There are many old workings, the remains of an old railway line down Strath Suardal, and quarries through Torrin by the shores of Loch Slapin. When the sun shines, the outcropping of the white marble below the waters of Loch Slapin reflects the light to produce wonderful colour in the sea loch. Once, this marble

OPPOSITE: The view south-west from Marsco to Gars-bheinn (left), Clach Glas (the Matterhorn-shaped peak in the centre, surprisingly unnamed on the 1:50,000 Ordnance Survey map) and, to the north, the face of the mighty Bla Bheinn (right). To add to the magic, minutes before I took this photograph a golden eagle took to the air a few feet in front of us – appropriately, for Marsco is said to come from Norse and means bird or seagull mountain.

OVERLEAF: A spring evening over Loch Ainort and Meall a' Mhaoil, looking to the twin tops of Glamaig.

was highly prized; it was even, it is said, used in the building of the Palace of Versailles. Although it is still quarried, its main use today seems to be as road aggregate for stabilising passing places on single-track roads.

This area provides a great deal of opportunity, with much to do at high and low levels. On the heights, the tough and demanding ridge traverse over Clach Glas to Bla Bheinn provides one of the best mountaineering experiences to be had on the whole of the island (graded Difficult). The Loch Slapin face of Bla Bheinn, known to climbers as the East Face, holds a feast of rock climbing routes, varying from the classic Great Prow (graded Very Severe) to the incredible blank-looking vertical wall of Stairway To Heaven (Graded E5). For many, the ordinary walk up the 'munro' of Bla Bheinn will be challenging enough! Outside the mountains, the sandstone sea cliffs of Elgol can be climbed most of the year.

The Red Cuillin, with the distinctly shaped peaks of Glamaig, Marsco and Beinn na Caillich, is particulary noted for its many fine walks. The weather is notably more reliable that in the Black Cuillin; quite often, all the tops will be visible and walkable when it is lashing down on the other side of Glen Sligachan. Low-level walks are abundant and of all grades of difficulty. In particular, a linear walk (car pick-up essential) through Glen Sligachan and on to Elgol is a favourite route through a key wilderness area.

BELOW: Clach Glas (great stone), seen from Gars-bheinn; it is known to mountaineers as the Matterhorn of Skye. After starting from the shores of Loch Slapin and ascending Sgurr nan Each, the Clach Glas to Bla Bheinn traverse offers one of the best mountaineering scrambles in Britain, demanding in both ascent and descent.

BELOW: The full extent of the Clach Glas to Bla Bheinn traverse is revealed in this aspect, taken from the top of nearby Marsco.

RIGHT: Extensive broken red granite scree and the sweeping flanks of hills well express the gentle nature of the Red Cuillin. This is the scene looking north-west from Gars-bheinn to the tops of Beinn Dearg first, then to Beinn Dearg Mhor, with the twin tops of Glamaig seen either side beyond. The narrows of Raasay gleam in the background.

BELOW: Among fine-grained red granite, Moss Campion (Silene acaulis) grows above Bealach Beiste on Gars-bheinn.

BELOW: From Marsco to Beinn
Dearg Mheadhonach with Sgurr
Mhairi (the west top of Glamaig)
peeping over the rounded ridge
of Druim na Ruaige. Beginning
from the Sligachan Hotel, a
horseshoe route up Beinn Dearg
via the ridge of Druim na Ruaige
and finishing over Glamaig is
one of the classic outings in the
Red Cuillin.

RIGHT: The road from Broadford to Elgol leads through the hamlet of Torrin, revealing this magnificent view of Bla Bheinn over the turquoise waters of Loch Slapin. The intense colour of the water is due to the reflection of the light from the underlying rocks of white marble.

OVERLEAF: From the east coast road, between Broadford and the Sligachan Hotel, this view over Loch Ainort and beyond the village of Luib reveals some of the hills of the Red Cuillin. Left stands Marsco with, to the right, the lesser bump of Ciche na Bheinne Deirge leading to Beinn Dearg Mheadhonach, which is in turn attached to Beinn Dearg, though it is difficult see the join. The flanks of Beinn Dearg Mhor fall to the far right. The Gaelic names here are easy to translate: Beinn Dearg means 'red hill'; Mheadhonach is 'middle' and Mhor 'biggest'.

BELOW: Beyond the Sligachan Hotel, the shapely peak of Marsco from this aspect has been compared to a knight's helmet. To the left, the pointed knife-blade of Clach Glas protrudes menacingly above the flank of Gars-bheinn. Pioneer climbers, before the benefit of motor transport, would begin their day from the Sligachan Hotel. To walk to Clach Glas, and the even more distant north face of Bla Bheinn, required starting at around 4 a.m. – long days in the hills indeed. Today we simply drive around to Loch Slapin on the far side of the Red Cuillin.

BELOW: Artists make a study of the Sligachan Hotel and the Black Cuillin beyond. The old arched bridge leads from the Red to the Black Cuillin side of the Sligachan River. The strategically placed 'Sliggy' remains a popular base for climbers and walkers, as it nestles amid the mountains and lies beside the road leading north to Portree and the great sea cliffs of Trotternish.

BELOW: The path leading down the eastern side of the long and lonely Glen Sligachan – the valley that separates the Red Cuillin and Strathaird from the Black Cuillin – passes directly beneath the toe of Marsco (to the left) and by the entrance to the Harta Corrie and the Bloody Stone (unseen, to the right) before splitting. The right fork then climbs over the end of the great Druim nan Ramh, seen here directly beyond the tiny lochan, to fall to Loch Coruisk. The left fork leads on down to the coast by the cottages of Camasunary.

OPPOSITE: This study of Marsco clearly shows that steep, unbroken granite is to be found among the hills of the Red Cuillin. Fictan Dearg is the steep crag looking out west over Glen Sligachan, and it sports a number of rock climbs. The first was ascended by Noell Odell in 1943, the last man to see Mallory and Irvine alive on Everest during their ill-fated 1924 expedition. My favourite way to ascend Marsco is by the north-west shoulder, utilising the deep gully rising diagonally from the bottom right of this photograph. At the head of the gully, exposed scrambling leads up to a final section of sharp-edged ridge.

BELOW: A moody afternoon of sunshine and showers over Lower Breakish and the islands of Pabay and Scalpay. Broadford Bay lies to the left and the great bulk of Beinn na Caillich (732m), famed for its huge stone summit cairn – it is of such a size that it can be plainly seen from the streets of Broadford below. Legend says that a 'Norwegian princess' is buried beneath it – 'Saucy Mary' perchance? It is more likely to be prehistoric. Thomas Pennant climbed this mountain in 1772, and described the scene to the west as 'that of desolation itself; a savage series of rude mountains, discoloured black and red, as if by the rage of fire.'

LEFT: North over Loch Eishort and the little island of Eilean Ruairidh is the entrance to Loch Slapin with its surrounding hills of Strathaird and the Red Cuillin. This view is taken from the north coast of the Sleat Peninsula, from within the ruins of Dunscaith Castle, where the legendary Irish warrior-hero Cuchullin once stayed to eye up the distant mountains.

BELOW: Over the head of Loch Ainort to the Beinn Deargs, the mountain grasses and the heather take on the burnt gold of autumn.

BELOW: By Glamaig, heliotrope skies herald a new dawn.

OVERLEAF: Over Loch Slapin, looking west to mighty Bla Bheinn (928m), left, with Clach Glas standing centrally. Though situated in the region of Strathaird, Bla Bheinn is built of erosion-resistant gabbro, like the Black Cuillin. Along with its sheer size and power, it has many spectacular features: steep cliffs, soaring towers and knife-edge ridges. Many feel it is the finest mountain on Skye.

OPPOSITE: Eas a' Bhradain waterfall lies just above the head of Loch Ainort above the main road to the Sligachan Hotel. Melting winter snows help feed the flow which on many occasions reaches quite stunning proportions. A nearby lay-by allows motorists to stop and take a closer look. But take care not to slip – there are no safeguards.

BELOW: A layer of ice grips the rushes growing in Loch Cill Chriosad.

BELOW: Glamaig and the peak of Sgurr Mhairi, plastered in snow. Under these conditions, a ski descent looks highly inviting.

BELOW: Marsco with a thin topping of cloud and the knife-edge ridge of Clach Glas and Bla Bheinn beyond.

weather and the seasons

It can be very wet on the Isle of Skye, particularly over the Black Cuillin. Not for nothing goes the old mountaineers' adage: 'If you can't see the tops it's raining, if you can see them it's going to rain!' However, the weather in each area can be, and usually is, completely different. When it is teeming down in the Black Cuillin, Duirinish or Trotternish can be bathed in sunshine. Even closer than this, I have experienced on numerous occasions that rain and cloud can be hanging over Sgurr nan Gillean and the rest of the Black Cuillin, yet on the other side of Glen Sligachan the Red Cuillin is perfectly dry.

My advice is be flexible – it's pointless having fixed ideas about walking or climbing in the Black Cuillin if it's pouring down. If you are being stormlashed in Glen Brittle then move to another area – there is an abundance of climbing and walking in all the regions. It is my experience that the weather on Skye is too complex to predict reliably. If you are planning a trip to the island, just go – don't be put off by a poor forecast. Anything can happen, and whatever is happening changes very quickly.

The next thing to consider is when to go. Again, there is no fixed answer. The rules on Skye are simply made for breaking. The climate is classed as maritime and it is most influenced by the sea. Prevailing westerlies running over the Minch are predominant. These winds usually carry clouds heavy in moisture which mostly shed their load on the highest mountains, the Black Cuillin. Seasons on Skye are more subtle and blurred around the edges than elsewhere, but they do exist.

Spring is definitely the awakening month. Warmth floods over the island, flowers open and begin to bloom, birds nest and butterflies fly and all the greenery begins to unfold. May is usually the pleasantest and most representative month of spring. Snow can linger on the Black Cuillin long into the month, but the weather is often at its best. Skye is close enough to the Arctic Circle for daylight hours to be very long; those with reasonable eyesight can read a paper at 11 p.m. by natural light (maybe you can at midnight too, but I'm usually asleep by then!). Another consideration, hugely important for those camping or using the outdoors, is that the tiny angel of misery, the midge, has not yet emerged in significant numbers.

August, the month of purple heather, is when most people visit Skye. It can be hot and sunny. You could have a dip in Loch Brittle and experience the first gatherings of the Arctic salmon on their way back to their spawning grounds. But sea winds can blow, lowering the temperature, and rain can engulf the mountains. Remember, however, to enjoy just one day of sunshine among the Black Cuillin is priceless. And surely there will be one!

September is one of my favourite months on the island. The mountain grasses begin to colour wonderfully and the weather can be nicely settled. I have climbed in the high Black Cuillin during this month, although there is usually a cold edge to the wind and the fingers quickly begin to numb. On the sea cliffs, however, particularly those of the east coast, Kilt Rock, Staffin and Flodigarry and Rubha Hunish in the far north, sheltered

ABOVE: Not long wet, not long dry: the ever-changing light on Skye makes it a photographer's paradise, portraying sunshine and showers, lovely rainbows and moody seascapes. This view is south along the east coast cliffs of Trotternish, from the Kilt Rock viewing area. Throughout the long coastline, prevailing westerlies blow both fair and foul weather. The east coast generally remains the driest, since the intervening mountains and high lands absorb most of the precipitation. Rock climbers should note that the sea cliffs of Trotternish often remain climbable when those on the west coast are lashed by rain and gale.

RIGHT: *Of course, the exception proves the rule! The Falls of Mealt, by the Kilt Rock viewpoint, are here being blown backwards over the top of the cliff by a strong easterly. I took this shot looking south from the top of Kilt Rock while clinging to the heather as best I could. The cliffs below the viewpoint are plumb vertical; under normal conditions, the waterfall free-falls for some 55m to the rocky beach below.*

from the westerlies, conditions can be positively balmy. September has also, for me, been the best month for experiencing the magical phenomena of the Northern Lights, the *Aurora Borealis*.

Winter is possibly best represented by March. It could be bleak and wet, or conversely the mountains could be plastered in snow. During 2006 the schoolchildren of Portree were sledging for weeks on end, though it is remarkably rare for snow to linger anywhere but on the heights. At some stage in winter, often during this month as the days begin to lengthen, it is feasible to make a traverse of the main ridge of the Black Cuillin in truly Alpine conditions – when it is plastered in snow and ice. The dream of every British mountaineer, this feat was first accomplished in February 1965 by Hamish McInnes, the incomparable Tom Patey, with Davie Crab and Brian Robertson.

Irrespective of season, it is worth emphasising just how unpredictable and changeable the weather can be. Within the blink of an eye, conditions can vary from flat calm to howling gale. On the high tops, snow can fall in early summer and the sun shine in the depths of winter. In the Black Cuillin I have been in snowstorms during May and June and severely chilled by high winds. A short time later, the sun has come out and it is necessary to strip off all my outer layers of clothing! Whether it looks like sunshine or showers, my advice is simple: catch the moment.

the black cuillin

There are many with a passion for mountains and climbing for whom the whole of Skye amounts to one thing only: the Black Cuillin. For pure naked rock sweeping from sea level to an altitude of some 1,000m, for jagged peaks and pinnacles, huge unbroken vertical faces, plunging rock slabs, long notched knife-edged ridges – there is nowhere else like it. To scale the heights, solve the challenges of its many steep places, explore its complexities and traverse its long ridges is the stuff of dreams.

The Cuillin has a magnetism and a spiritual dimension which goes far beyond its physical form. Sometimes after a day's climbing I have lingered among these heights watching the sky turn purple, the moon rise, the stars appear one by one, just listening to the awesome silence – staying to savour the feeling that the best thing about the day was not the climb, nor the fun or laughter, but just being there, to be absorbed by and somehow part of the Cuillin. There is a power in these mountains, a timelessness that says: 'We, the Cuillin, are inviolate, we represent how things should be, we are a piece of God-given perfection available free, forever, to anyone who asks.'

> Long, long and distant,
> long the ascent.
> long the way of the Cuillin
> and the peril of your striving . . .
>> Sorley MacLean, 'The Cuillin'

Imagine, then, the reaction when in 2000 the late clan chief John MacLeod of Macleod not only claimed ownership of these mountains, but put them up for sale. Legally it was a doubtful claim, and many thought simply that no man had the right to claim ownership of mountains, especially the Cuillin. Had the old injustices returned? Could the rich land-owning classes simply toy with the freedom and aspirations of others at their own choosing? Let us hope this particular storm has passed not to return. John MacLeod died in 2007 with his claim widely contended, and the future uncertain for Dunvegan Castle.

The Cuillin is defined to the east by Glen Sligachan and to the west by Glen Brittle. At its northern head stands the Sligachan Hotel; its southern foot falls into Soay Sound. The southernmost top is Gars-bheinn (895m); the northernmost, the most visible, is the magnificent Sgurr nan Gillean (965m). The highest top is Sgurr Alasdair (993m). Between them is a paradise of bare rock and mountains.

The Cuillin forms a great horseshoe of peaks joined by long, serrated, narrow rock ridges, some 12km in length. The heart of the cirque lies to the east of the massif, with its lonely Loch Coruisk. Great hanging corries scallop the flanks of the chain either side of the central ridge, defined by a host of side ridges which run off the main ridge. Naturally, to traverse the main Cuillin Ridge has always been one of the most sought-after prizes in British mountaineering.

Although the first peaks in the Cuillin were being climbed in the 1800s – Sgurr nan Gillean in 1836 and Sgurr Alasdair in 1873 – it was not until after a period of intense development by the Alpinists of the day that the possibility of a complete traverse of the Cuillin Ridge was considered. Norman Collie, one of the foremost climbing pioneers of the late nineteenth century who did great things all round the British mountains, the Alps, the Canadian Rockies and even the Himalayan giant Nanga Parbat, was utterly defeated by the Cuillin Ridge. Ashley Abraham, whose seminal work *Rock Climbing In Skye* was published in 1908, thought it could never be done in one continuous expedition; it was unlikely, he declared, that any single man could possess the necessary 'exceptional physique', 'staying power' and 'intimate knowledge of the entire range'.

The experts were quickly proved wrong when Leslie Shadbolt and Alastair McLaren made the first continuous traverse of the main ridge on 10 June 1911. Both skilled rock climbers,

OPPOSITE: Rising from the sea, from the Isle of Mists, is the magnificent, incomparable Black Cuillin. This view from Loch Scavaig looks north over the foot of Loch Coruisk, at the heart of the Black Cuillin, to the pyramidal pinnacle of Sgurr nan Gillean, the north-eastern terminus of the great Black Cuillin ridge. The mountain in the right foreground is Sgurr na Stri and the middle ground is formed by the long subsidiary ridge of Druim nan Ramh.

they had climbed together in the Cuillin for a number of years, and planned their expedition with great care. Their time between the two end summits of Gars-bheinn and Sgurr nan Gillean was a remarkable 12 hours 18 minutes (the whole trip, from and to valley level, took a shade under 18 hours). It was a remarkable feat of ability and daring, and their time was respectable even by modern standards.

Geology and subsequent periods of glaciation shaped the Cuillin into what we see now. After the great magma mass cooled slowly to produce the crystalline gabbro, the upper layers were removed by subsequent periods of erosion. But that is far from the whole story: as any climber will tell you, the rocks of the Cuillin are not all immaculately rough gabbro. Another rock was produced along with the gabbro: peridotite. Many boulders of this rock are found lying on the glaciated slabs near Loch Coruisk. Typically, it weathers to produce a rough pitted surface of a distinct brown turning to orange.

Throughout the whole mass basalt and dolerite, dykes and intrusions have penetrated the gabbro. These run in a number of directions and over time have weathered at a different rate

from the gabbro. This process explains the deep gullies and notches that cut through the ridges and define the peaks. Generally, these dykes and intrusions are much more slippery, particularly in the wet, and often crumblier than the gabbro.

Although weathering of the rocks is a continuous process, the greatest effect on the scene as we see it today was the glaciation of the massif by the Cuillin Icefield around 10,500 years ago. As the ice flowed away from the centre, it left the main ridge, with the lesser ridges, enclosing the ice-scalloped hanging basins and corries, falling away from it. Where the gabbro rocks have been scoured by the ice they are generally smooth and integral and, typically in the corrie floors, form great whaleback-shaped outcrops. However, the high peaks, nunataks, which protruded above the last ice cap are often frost-shattered and it is not unusual to find areas of precariously piled loose blocks. Add to all this the many variations in the gabbro itself, and it will be understood that the rocks of the Cuillin require thoughtful management by all those enjoy walking and climbing on them.

OVERLEAF: Fishing boats off the jetty at Elgol, with the backdrop of the Black Cuillin. The mountain topped by cloud on the left is Gars-bheinn (misspelled on the 1:50,000 Ordnance Survey map!) and over to the right stands the point of Sgurr nan Gillean. In between these tops stretches the great horseshoe spine of the Black Cuillin ridge – some 13km of jagged peaks connected by a long rock ridge, knife-edged in places.

BELOW: Looking north-west from the lower slopes of Sgurr na Stri to the head of Loch Coruisk gives a wild and rocky aspect. The far central mountain is Sgurr a' Ghreadaidh whose high North Top stands at 973m and whose name (pronounced 'Sgurr Greeta') translates as 'Peak of Thrashings' – perhaps a reference to its frequent battering by the prevailing winds. The peak prominent in the left foreground is Sgurr Dubh Beag. The long east ridge profiled here, falling from its summit to the shore of Loch Coruisk, is known to climbers as the Dubh Slabs. It provides a clean, glacially cut sweep of rock ascending for over a kilometre; technically easy and usually ascended unroped, it is considered to be one of the longest and finest in Britain.

OPPOSITE: Capturing the loneliness and rocky desolation of Loch Coruisk, this view looks out from the cliffs of Coir-uisg Buttress, on the lower slopes of Sgurr a' Ghreadaidh, down to the foot of Loch Coruisk. The peak is Sgurr na Stri and beyond can be seen the coast of the Strathaird Peninsula over the sea waters of Loch Scavaig.

BELOW: The great rock face of Sron na Ciche, lit by evening sun. Easily accessible from the campsite in Glen Brittle, this is the most popular climbing cliff in the whole of the Black Cuillin. Some 300m in height, it stretches for over a kilometre in length.

OPPOSITE: A snowstorm in May on the summit of Sgurr nan Gillean. After I had ascended the snow-bedecked Pinnacle Ridge, the sun seemed to be breaking through a thin layer of cloud – then, suddenly, the air filled with feather-like swirling flakes of snow. It was a magical experience, as if unseen gods above were having a pillow fight. These perched blocks top the West Ridge; quite a few people ascending to the summit squeeze through the obvious hole here.

BELOW: Swirling cloud, not uncommon hereabouts, around the rocky summit spire of Sgurr nan Gillean. To the left lies the Pinnacle Ridge, with the Knight's Peak (4th pinnacle) just visible in the cloud; to the right, the West Ridge falls to Am Basteir. This photograph was taken from Sgurr a' Bhasteir, reached on this occasion by an abseil descent down King's Cave Chimney on the Sligachan side of the Bhasteir Tooth. Sgurr nan Gillean is a climb suitable only for highly competent mountaineers.

BELOW: From this position, the
path leading from the base of the
Coire a' Bhasteir basin, the main
features of the Pinnacle Ridge
are revealed to good effect.
I included the Pinnacle Ridge
in my book Great British Ridge
Walks, though I was careful
to explain that it is definitely a
climb and not just a walk. It just
seemed too good to leave out!
There are four distinct 'pinnacles',
with the 3rd pinnacle being the
most difficult to traverse. From
its top, descent into the gap
below, separating it from the
Knight's Peak, is usually made
by roped abseil.

BELOW: The Cioch area of the huge cliffs of Sron na Ciche, viewed from the upper basin of Coire Lagan. The deep gully, seen centrally in this image, is Eastern Gully. The Cioch (breast) protrudes to its right, made proud by the fact that it is throwing a shadow – exactly as it was first discovered by Norman Collie and local man John Mackenzie, who went on to climb it in 1906.

RIGHT: Looking across the hanging basin of Coir a' Ghrunnda from the col of Bealach a' Garbh-choire (a bealach is the pass or col between peaks), sited beneath the mountain of Sgurr nan Eag. The highest peaks opposite are first, to the left, Sgurr Sgumain with the snow patches beneath, and to its right, separated by a scree-filled notch, Sgurr Alasdair. Although not obvious in this image, Sgurr Alasdair is the higher, in fact the highest mountain in Skye, at 993m. The photograph was taken near the southern start of the great traverse of the Black Cuillin ridge, the point at which those attempting it are most likely to ask, 'What have I let myself in for?' I have been in this position twice! Ahead lie much endeavour, great exposure, many difficulties and, for a few, the sweet feeling of success.

OVERLEAF: A revealing view looking west from Sgurr nan Each in the Red Cuillin, along the full length of the Black Cuillin ridge; the cone of Sgurr nan Eag lies to the left and the pyramid of Sgurr nan Gillean to the right. The ridge involves some 26 different tops, 22km of distance (12km along the ridge plus 10km to get on and off it from the road) and around 4,000m of ascent. A successful traverse requires fair weather, sound judgement and a high degree of mountaineering ability. Exposure is high throughout the traverse, but several key sections are steeper and more challenging than the rest, involving technical rock climbing. A few places also present particularly complicated route-finding challenges. Not for nothing is the Black Cuillin ridge regarded as the finest mountaineering expedition in the British Isles.

LEFT: Glacier-mint waters pour down Harta Corrie.

RIGHT: This fine waterfall tumbles from the high-hanging basin of Lota Corrie down into Harta Corrie below. The overlooking peaks are Sgurr na Bhairnich to the left and the shapely Bruach na Frithe to the right. Mountain artist Ginger Cain considers the Harta and Lota Corries to be among the most spectacular in the whole of Skye.

LEFT: As the road descends to Glen Brittle, a great corrie, with views to the north-western peaks of the Black Cuillin, opens to the left. This is Coire na Creiche and the dominant feature at its head, below the topmost heights of the ridge, is the huge buttress of Sgurr an Fheadain, riven down its centre by the tremendous rift of Waterpipe Gully. Not so noticeable from this distance, though also bearing testimony to the power of the water which flows down this basin, are the little waterfalls that feed the Fairy Pools of the Allt Coir a' Mhadaidh burn. Through solid volcanic bedrock, the water has smoothed out an intriguing series of runlets and pools that belie the ground's hardness and strength.

RIGHT: On a hot summer's day, when it would be folly indeed to rush to the barren heights, the enchanting emerald-green Fairy Pools at the base of Coire na Creiche can stop climbers in their tracks. They are deep, cold and refreshing. Have a care, though: one in particular has an underwater bar of resistant dolerite which arches under the water's surface like a suspended girder supporting some structure invisible to the human eye.

BELOW: A red sky ends the day over the north-west terminus of the Black Cuillin. Sgurr nan Gillean is to the left and Bruach na Frithe to the right.

OPPOSITE: Starbreak over the Cuillin mountains, from the road leading over the moor from Carbost to Glen Brittle. No filters were needed to achieve this effect, just a small aperture and a fast shutter speed (blink your eyes rapidly at the sun and you will get the same effect). The highest peak to the right is Sgurr a' Ghreadaidh.

OVERLEAF: Sgurr nan Gillean, reflected in Loch nan Eilean beside the road leading to the west from the Sligachan Hotel. I stopped in the early morning to take this image after an all-night drive from my home in the Lake District to climb on Sron na Ciche.

BELOW: Loch an Fhir-bhallaich, beside the path from Glen Brittle campsite to Sron na Ciche. The far path above the shore rises directly from the youth hostel. It is October, the mountain grasses are rapidly turning golden-brown and a squally wind darkens the blue surface of the lochan – on the crag it will be cold on the fingers. All too soon, there will be no more rock climbing on Sron na Ciche for another five months.

OPPOSITE: Evening falls over Loch an Fhir after a long day spent on the delectable cliffs of Sron na Ciche. Some days, when the moon is risen and lights the descent, it is so still that all you hear is the sound of the waves running up, and back down, the pebble beach of Glen Brittle far below, regularly crashing and sucking like the sound of a sleeping giant's breath.

OVERLEAF: Caught as the sun creeps above the Sleat Peninsula, the first red light of a winter's morn reveals a dusting of snow on Gars-bheinn. This is a classic much-photographed view from Elgol, showing the south-western tip of the Black Cuillin.

BELOW: Looking south-east over Loch Harport and the little community of Portnalong, this striking view shows a remarkable profile of the northern and central Black Cuillin garbed in the white snows of winter. The mountain on the far left is Glamaig in the Red Cuillin, but the massif to the right is Bruach na Frithe above Fionn Corrie. Following this are the tops around Coire na Creiche, Coire a' Ghreadaidh and Coir an Eich, ending with the top of Sgurr na Banachdich falling in a long shoulder towards Sgurr nan Gobhar (the top of which is just out of the frame).

BELOW: 'The British Alps': over Glen Brittle, from the heights of Beinn Staic, to the corries of Coir' an Eich (left) and Coire na Banachdich (right), all of which lie within the central Black Cuillin. The tops, falling from the mighty Sgurr na Banachdich at the head of Coir' an Eich, are An Diallaid (left) and Sgurr nan Gobhar (right). Over Coire na Banachdich the heights of Sgurr Dearg rise into the clouds, with the dark mass of Window Buttress on the edge of the corrie below.

OVERLEAF: There are various interpretations, both Norse and Gaelic, of the names of the tops that occupy the northern end of the Black Cuillin, seen here above the Sligachan Hotel. The pyramidal spire of Sgurr nan Gillean to the left could mean 'Peak of Gills' in Norse, a gill being a ravine or steep gully, or 'Peak of the Young Men' in Gaelic. To the right, shrouded in light cloud, is Am Basteir, with the distinct pinnacle of the Bhasteir Tooth sticking out to its right; this is from the Gaelic and means 'the Executioner', obviously referring to the outline of the Bhasteir Tooth like an executioner's axe. Sgurr a' Bhasteir forms the distinct right triangular-shaped peak, with its long diagonal flank sweeping left to underscribe Am Basteir. Surely this has something of Zen and Japanese art about it: Zen points directly to the human heart, and this is simply the most sublime skyline I know.

flora and fauna

LEFT: My climbing companion Luke Steer and I were wading through the sea at low tide to reach a climb called Supercharger, on the dramatic cliffs of Neist Point above Moonen Bay on the west coast of Duirinish. Things were not going well – the water level was much higher than anticipated – when I suddenly realised we were surrounded by jellyfish. Not one or two, but a multitude. To say my reaction was one of mild panic would be fair, though I did manage to take this photograph on my faithful Rollei 35 slung high around my neck. Subsequent examination of the image revealed that it was the Common Moon Jellyfish: a configuration of four pink-purple eyes at the centre make it unmistakeable. For the record, it is harmless, non-stinging, to man. Reputedly.

Every drop of rain that falls upon mountain and moor, that runs over and under the ground on its way to the sea, produces and sustains life. Needless to say, the diversity and richness of habitat, of flora and fauna, on and around Skye is quite breathtaking: it is of world importance. Of course, it is not just the fact that life-giving rainfall is plentiful – a major factor, particularly in plant biodiversity, is the wonderfully varied geology of the area both within and throughout the individual regions.

Plants

There are plenty of peat bogs around Skye and the plants on them tend to be common throughout the whole area. The sweet-smelling bog myrtle is such a plant – most people who walk by and accidentally crush its leaves will recognise its familiar scent. Crushed and smeared, it is held to be a deterrent to the voracious midge, but personally I cannot claim any success – if anything, the biting midge seems to be rather attracted to it! Not all the bog plants are common: the bog moss *Sphagnum skyense* is unique to Strath Suardal.

The limestones, particularly of Strathaird and Strath Suardal, hold a remarkable collection of plants. My favourite, abundant on the flanks of Ben Suardal, is mountain avens. A rarity is the long-leaved helleborine, a large white orchid. Protected from the grazing of sheep and cattle, hidden in the grykes (limestone fissures), grows dark red helleborine. Typical of the wind-blasted Red Cuillin are the flattened plants of juniper. In protected gullies there is some variety, including the lovely primrose in springtime.

On the heights of the Black Cuillin, nutrients and minerals are reluctant to leave the hard matrix of the gabbro rock, yet plants do grow even in these difficult conditions. Northern rockcress thrives and the alpine rockcress finds its only home here outside the European Alps. Overall, the heights of Trotternish provide the richest environment for plant species. For a wonderful array of alpines, observe the inaccessible, therefore ungrazed, tops of the pinnacles surrounding the Table amid the Quirang landslip. No climbing is necessary as the Table overlooks a lower pinnacle. A very special plant hereabouts is the Arctic Iceland purslane; its only other British home is on the not-too-distant Island of Mull.

Birds

Again, diversity of habitat makes the island one of the best locations in Europe for wealth and variety of bird life. It is difficult to know just where to begin. Looking down from the heights, there is little to compare with the sight of a golden eagle soaring effortlessly up on a thermal – up, up and away in a matter of seconds. Skye has one of the densest populations of golden eagles in Europe. Nevertheless, its grip on survival is tentative; it would not take a great deal to destroy the necessary delicate balance irrevocably. The golden eagle nests between March and August: should you discover an eyrie during this critical time, please move on quickly and keep as low a profile as possible. Recent applications for a number of wind farms on the island are a cause of some concern: if these ventures are successful, many fear for the survival of the eagle.

The sea eagle, or white-tailed eagle, is a huge bird, and the Isle of Skye was once its last stronghold in Scotland. Due to persecution by the great hunting and shooting estates, its numbers rapidly declined and it last bred on Skye in 1916; it had completely disappeared by 1930. Recently, due to the efforts of the RSPB, it has been successfully reintroduced. It is breeding again and its numbers are slowly growing, which is very welcome news.

Other birds of prey, spread throughout the island, include peregrine falcon, merlin, hen harrier, buzzard, rough-legged buzzard and kestrel. Diving birds are spread across loch and sea, and include all the throated divers: red, black and great.

BELOW: A flight of oystercatchers, dazzling with their long white wingbars, flashed passed me at Staffin Slip on the east coast of Trotternish. Moments before, they had been pulling up earthworms with their striking orange-red beaks on the greensward above the rocky beach. The richness and variety of birdlife here, from the high mountains to the wild coast, are a feast for the senses.

RIGHT: Throughout the seasons, the shrill piping call and the striking coloration of oystercatchers are common around the shores of Skye. This group probes the mud and seaweed on a tide ebbing from the beach of Loch Portree.

Medium to small birds range through many species from ring ouzel to siskin.

Seabird colonies are healthy at the time of writing, with an amazing variety all around the coast, especially on the sea cliffs. Waders, ringed plovers and oystercatchers inhabit the shoreline, while many different gulls take to the air and float on the sea. Raven and fulmer nest on the sea cliffs, as do many other species such as cormorant, shag, guillemot, razorbill, black-backed razorbill and many more. Rubha Hunish and Neist Point are tremendous locations to view seabirds and their nesting habitats. I once saw a solitary puffin on Neist Point, although I am assured they do not breed there. Likewise, the startling dive of the gannet is a common sight, although they too do not supposedly nest at these locations.

Animals and fish

The red fox is allegedly common, though red deer are less so. The tiny common shrew inhabits many of the cliff tops and is best found by sitting and listening for its high-pitched whistle as it forages, seemingly non-stop, through heather and grass. Along the coastline, otters are supposedly common though rarely seen. Once on Flodigarry Island, unobserved from the heights of the cliffs, I looked down to see an otter carry a great Atlantic salmon on to a boulder and proceed to eat it.

Seals, both common and grey, live around the coast of the island and a fascinating variety of marine life can be observed in the sea. Probably the only way most will see lobsters, langoustine and octopus is when they are landed by lobster boats. However, all around the island, at various times of the year, dolphin, porpoise, bottlenose whale, minke whale, killer whale and basking shark are not uncommon.

The wild Atlantic salmon, netted under licence between Flodigarry and Staffin Islands, is in decline, yet still runs from around the end of August to September. It travels from the sea up the rivers to the gravel-bed spawning grounds near the foot of the mountains. The salmon's four-year journey from hatching to return is one of the wonders of the natural world. In the lochs and the rivers, brown trout still jump for the fly and in a number of lochs a bird from the last Ice Age remains – the Arctic char.

I have highlighted a mere fraction of the wonderful natural world of the Isle of Skye. Thankfully, it is still reasonably intact and remains to enrich all. Its survival is delicately balanced, small changes can have drastic and far-reaching consequences, and recently man's influence has started to take noticeable effect.

climbers operate a voluntary ban on going near nesting sites between May and July. Fulmers are masters of the air, wheeling and gliding over cliffs and sea with perfect control, even in gale-force winds. Like ace fighter-pilots, they can pass inches from your head while giving you a look which seems to say, 'This is my world – watch it.'

FAR RIGHT: Patient and silent, a grey heron stands motionless by the banks of the River Drynoch before striking with deadly speed to claim another fish. Fish, both salt and freshwater, and even frogs on marshy ground, are all fair game for this large, gangly bird.

OPPOSITE: The plant life of the island adds another dimension to the natural cornucopia of Skye. Clockwise from top left: Pink Purslane beneath bushes by the roadside near Dun Beag, Duirinish; Marsh Marigold at Waternish; Sea Thrift by Loch Dunvegan, Duirinish; Rowan flowers in May above Glen Drynoch.

RIGHT: A range of colourful autumn fungi near Skeabost. The central image is possibly Hygrocybe splendidissima.

BELOW: Winter Snowdrops flourish in the sheltered woods north of Portree Harbour.

trotternish

OPPOSITE: Looking from the head of the Staffin–Uig Pass into the great landslip feature of the Quirang, one of the largest known such slips in Britain. The rocky bastion, some way below the main cliffs, is commonly referred to in guidebooks as the Prison. This feature, formed from basalt lavas, once stood with the other cliffs high above, until the weaker underlying sedimentary rocks collapsed and the Prison slipped down the hillside.

OPPOSITE, BELOW LEFT: Underlying the volcanic lavas and hard dolerite sills of Trotternish are softer sedimentary rocks of Jurassic origin. These are rich in a variety of fossils formed from the creatures that lived here around 200 million years ago. Seen here are remnants of the ribbed spiral of an ammonite, an elaborately coiled squid-like creature.

OPPOSITE, BELOW RIGHT: Two figures beside the path to the inner sanctuary of the Quirang give a sense of scale to this dramatic feature known as the Needle. It was formed the same way as the Prison – by sliding down the hillside on its base of soft sedimentary rock after breaking away from the cap of hard volcanic rocks above.

OVERLEAF: Evening tones add depth to this scene looking north from Sconser Hotel over Balmeanach Bay to the outline of Ben Tianavaig and, in the far distance, the mountain of Storr.

When driving north towards Portree you may get a glimpse, on the distant horizon, of a weird-looking, free-standing 50m pinnacle, the Old Man of Storr. Plainly, despite all that has been observed on the journey so far – including the Red Cuillin and the Black Cuillin – there is a very different and fascinating world beyond. The wild windswept tracts of Trotternish, a land of mountains, moor, meadow and great sea cliffs, simply rewrite the rules of landscape, of desolation and deep, awesome beauty.

Trotternish is the final, most northerly and largest finger peninsula on the island, very much a world apart from all that has gone before. East is divided from west by the Trotternish Ridge, a ridge of mountains 32km long. The high point of this is the Storr (720m), which lies at the southern end and below whose massive cliffs stands the Old Man. High points along the ridge include Creag a' Lain (608m) and Beinn Edra (611m). North of the Staffin–Uig Pass the whole upland spine is headed by Meall na Suiramach (543m), which looks over the last point of Skye over the Minch to the distant Isle of Lewis. Despite its length, a walk along this chain of hills is not an arduous affair. You are constantly rewarded with superlative and ever-changing seascapes, and much of the going is on close-cropped greensward, akin to walking on a golf course.

The usual way to explore the region is to take the road north from Portree to pass beneath the Storr, then along the east coast to gain the community of Staffin with the huge landslip of the Quirang poised on the hillside of Meall na Suiramach above. The final leg continues beneath the striking white cliffs of Sron Vourlin and above the Flodigarry Hotel: the road is a little bumpy here because it's constantly on the move! Finally, it veers west to Duntulm. Return is made by motoring back down the west coast, first to Uig and then back to Portree. While this journey will give you a flavour of the region, it passes over much of what is fascinating about this outstanding area.

For me these are the mighty sea cliffs, a fraction of which can be glimpsed from the viewpoint looking to Kilt Rock from Loch Mealt. I have had much involvement with these cliffs, pioneering quite a few new climbs. One of my favourite areas to be in the world is on the headland of Rubha Hunish, the very northernmost tip of the island. I have a kind of fear-and-fascination relationship with this place – an emotion that is possibly only really understood by those who climb rocks for enjoyment. Here is a great headland horseshoe of 60m cliffs with a number of sea stacks standing off the lower peninsula below. For bird life, wildness and views out across untamed seas it has no equal.

The only real way to gain an understanding of this landscape, to appreciate its many and varied features, is to know a little about its geology and how it was formed. In a nutshell, this is a volcanic region built over sedimentary rocks. On the heights are the remnants of volcanic lavas known as plateau lavas. Mainly of these are amygdales which, when broken open, reveal mineralised nodules filled with white crystals. The type and quality of these lavas and basalts vary enormously, though generally speaking they are too rotten to climb on. Some bits are clearly more resistant than others, which explains why the Old Man of Storr and his surrounding courtiers stand alone – the softer surrounding rocks have been eroded away.

Below the heights are dolerite sills which were formed within the limestone itself. In this case, the underlying molten magma squeezed up into the limestones but did not make it to the surface. It cooled very slowly to form the great organ-pipe hexagonal columns that characterise these cliffs. Typically they give the appearance of pleats in a kilt, hence the name Kilt Rock for the cliffs below Ellishader and Loch Mealt. Erosion and glaciation again wore away the softer limestone above, leaving the cliffs to stand alone above the sea. However, in places, exposed at their feet, the sedimentary rocks remain.

BELOW: This is probably a small fossilised dinosaur footprint, implanted in the Jurassic mudstone slab outcropping on the beach of Staffin Bay. It appears to be one of a paired set of tracks, but unfortunately the others have been chiselled free of the bedding plane, leaving only damaged indents. Other larger and more impressive footprints have been officially verified in the near vicinity; they are thought to be around 200 million years old.

These sedimentary rocks are Jurassic in origin, and are made of sedimentary mudstones, sandstones and fossiliferous limestone. They are spectacularly rich in marine fossils, including bivalves, brachiopods (which appear as shells), the flat spirals of ammonites and long, bullet-like belemnites. Recently, the remains of reptiles, ichthyosaurs and plesiosaurs have been found, along with the vertebra and leg bones of different dinosaurs. In the shales and mudstones, fossilised plant remains and dinosaur footprints have also come to light. The little museum at Ellishader gives fascinating detail on all this and will point you in the right direction to go and look.

Another facet of this spectacular landscape are the huge landslips. These are the largest to be found in Britain and include the Fairy Glen above Uig, the hillside below the Storr and the most famous of them all – the Quirang above Staffin. A simple walk from the top of the Staffin–Uig Pass leads to the Quirang, and it is well worth close scrutiny. In the centre, enclosed by tottering pinnacles, is the remarkable dead-flat feature known as the Table – another of the amazing features which make the landscape of Trotternish unique.

BELOW: John Hargreaves makes a 'Tyrolean traverse' back to the mainland from Rubha Hunish, a rocky finger peninsula on the most northerly tip of Trotternish. On its east side are some exciting sea cliffs and three distinct sea stacks. On 11 June 1986, John and I made the first ascent of the South Stack. Climbing was the simple part – with heavy seas running, it was reaching and returning from the stack that were the interesting bits!

OPPOSITE: Looking east along the northern sea cliffs of Trotternish, over the complicated and spectacular geology of the dolerite cliffs of Bun-idein towards the hill of Ben Volovaig. The lower level of rock, plunging into the sea, is more compact and integral, while the upper layer, with a cockscomb appearance, is formed from columnar dolerite. The latter is found typically on Kilt Rock; here, it is twisted and radiates in a complicated three-dimensional pattern which makes its mode of formation particularly fascinating to interpret. Rock climbers looking for a challenge should note that these 90m cliffs are, at the time of writing, unclimbed. However, a word of warning: because of the pattern and varying angle of jointing of the rocks, the cliff looks decidedly unstable.

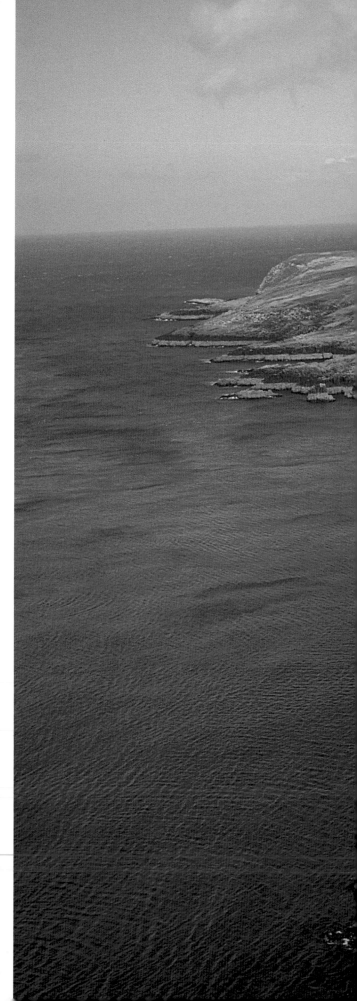

BELOW: This madcap climber – me! – is executing a 'Tyrolean traverse' to the top of Chimney Stack, prior to making the first ascent. On the cliffs north of Kilt Rock, this isolated free-standing column of dolerite rises from the sedimentary limestone below, separated from the main cliff by a 5m gap. Unusually, the ascent first required an abseil from the top to gain the base route on the seaward face. A grappling hook, thrown optimistically into the turf crowning the stack, secured the rope to make the crossing. The ascent proved even trickier than the approach. At the time, 1985, it was the most technically difficult climb on Skye.

OPPOSITE: Looking south to the silhouette of Chimney Stack strikingly illustrates the nature of the vertically jointed columnar dolerite, prevalent throughout the sea cliffs of Trotternish.

BELOW: Tranquil today, the scene looking north over Staffin Slip to Staffin and Flodigarry Islands. The white buildings of Flodigarry can be seen to the left of the second island, with the curve of Staffin Bay unseen to the left. The narrow strait between the slip and Staffin Island is still used to net, under licence, wild Atlantic salmon which chiefly run in late August and September. During the season, the nets are hung to dry on large poles outside the fishing station, the only building on the island. The distant skyline is shaped by the Isle of Lewis, the largest island of the Outer Hebrides. The radial pattern of 'lazy beds' in the foreground indicates the old 'runrig' system of agriculture, which has long disappeared from the Western Isles.

BELOW: The larger pinnacle here is the 50m Old Man of Storr. The lesser rock in the foreground, the nearest large pinnacle to the Old Man, standing between it and the main face of Storr, I call the Old Woman. The dominant Old Man has quite an entourage of pinnacles around him. The hollow between them and the cliff is known as the Sanctuary. This is another classic landslip area: all the pinnacles have slipped down from the cliffs above. Have a care here: the predominant rock type is a rather rotten basalt lava, and spontaneous rock falls from the immense cliffs of the Storr looming above are not uncommon. My advice is to keep out of the Sanctuary, for in fact it is anything but one.

BELOW: The ruined Duntulm Castle provides an eerie silhouette against the silver light of Loch Snizort, with the hills of Waternish beyond. The castle, once the chief seat of the MacDonalds of the Isles, is the subject of countless legends and alleged clan atrocities. It was finally abandoned in the 1700s. The site is very impressive, with the sheltered Tulm Bay offering a natural harbour of considerable strategic position. Above the bay, not named or detailed on the 1:50,000 Ordnance Survey map, is a great linear crofting community (now in ruins) and interspaced with this are much older foundations, burial mounds and evidence of prehistory. This has clearly been an important settlement site for thousands of years.

BELOW: The aspect north along the Trotternish ridge over Beinn Edra to the distant Quirang and the lower flat-topped Sron Vourlin. Trees play no part in this powerfully primeval, open, windswept landscape.

BELOW: South along the Trotternish ridge with Storr in the distance. The traverse of this long North Ridge of Skye is a very rewarding walk. Each part of the ridge, the eastern cliffs and corries and the surrounding lowlands have their own character; the unfolding seascapes are a constant delight. There are no technical difficulties; although the way is long (over 32km from the Uig–Staffin Pass to Portree), the walking is easy. It is possible to quit the ridge at a number of locations from a bealach (pass); one obvious choice, after ascending the Storr, is to descend from Bealach Beag, provided you have a car strategically placed by the roadside.

LEFT: Plunging directly into deep water, these exposed, wave-battered cliffs form the eastern edge of the Rubha Hunish peninsula. Its many rock ledges and turf topping provide an important nesting ground for considerable colonies of seabirds including fulmer, shag, cormorant, kittiwake, gannet, guillemot, razorbill and a variety of gulls. A pair of binoculars is a useful accessory here. I once watched a nuclear submarine, black and sinister, sail silently round this headland having completed its deep diving trials in the nearby Inner Sound. It was a bit of a surprise – Rubha Hunish is the sort of place that makes you forget the wider, less beautiful, world beyond.

BELOW: This is the middle sea stack which I climbed off the east coast of the Rubha Hunish peninsula, before I turned my attention to the great horseshoe of higher surrounding cliffs. The hill in the distance is Ben Volovaig, above the Aird. As yet the intervening sea cliffs seen here are all unclimbed. The bird life hereabouts is quite stunning but, as if this is not enough, one eye should also be kept on the sea. Porpoise, basking shark, killer, sperm and minke whales are not uncommon visitors to these remote shores.

OPPOSITE: The great sea eagle, persecuted to extinction on Skye, has recently been reintroduced – here it glides untroubled over its domain, despite being harried by a rather courageous herring gull. The last indigenous white-tailed eagle was reported to have nested on Skye in 1918 and the last lonely eagle was seen in 1930. In my early days of climbing on the Trotternish sea cliffs, before the eagle's successful reintroduction, Willie MacLeod of Duntulm frequently described to me the antics of nesting sea eagles on the cliffs of Rubha Hunish. So vivid were his descriptions, I thought he must have mistaken the common buzzard for the eagle, which puzzled me enormously. Eventually the penny dropped: with absolute clarity, Willie was recalling observations that were more than sixty years old.

OPPOSITE, BELOW: Despite the sheer size of the sea eagle – it has a wing span of some 2.5m – its mastery over its environment is astonishing. Here, after plunging from the heights above, it uses its huge talons to pluck a fish from the sea with hair's-breadth accuracy.

BELOW: On the southern edge of Trotternish, as the hills begin to rise towards the Storr and the central spine of the North Ridge, a rainbow points to a crock of gold somewhere in Borve.

BELOW: On the path to Rubha Hunish, starting from the telephone box at Duntulm, a long line of ruined crofts is passed – this is the last and most northerly. The arrangement is very distinctive, and looks similar to photographs of the abandoned township on distant St Kilda. Growing atop this long-abandoned wall is a lovely spread of ling heather, a common enough mountain shrub, perhaps, but nevertheless one of importance to the people who lived here. For agreeing to grow on mountains and moors where little else will grow, God gave the heather three great gifts. Strength: the bark of heather, stronger than that of any other plant or tree in the world, was used to thatch roofs and make ropes to lower people over nearby Rubha Hunish to take seabirds' eggs. Fragrance: heather has a honeysuckle-like perfume, and potpourris of it would be found in most dwellings. Finally, sweetness: heather blossom is a favourite for honey-producing bees.

OPPOSITE: The vague path leading to the far left corner of this image disappears behind a large marker boulder, to descend a stairway of steps cut into the rock. These steps and the path beyond provide the only safe way down through the cliffs of Rubha Hunish to the finger peninsula below (Duntulm resident Willie MacLeod once kept a small boat there). Below the rough ground on the clifftop lie the remnants of the burial mounds of a long-forgotten civilisation.

BELOW: Kilt Rock, viewpoint and picnic area, is the perfect place to view the vertical jointing – the pleats in the kilt – of the columnar dolerite which formed in horizontal layers between the sedimentary rocks. These cliffs are impressively vertical. The underlying bands of limestones, mudstones and sandstones are also clearly seen from this point. Rock climbing started here in earnest in 1983, and for those who like the challenge of scaling cracks and steep places this is an excellent place to climb.

OPPOSITE: My colleague Bob Wightman climbs behind me up the first ascent of a route we called Drop the Pilot, made in 1984. It follows the steep corner crack of a column out on a wall to the left of, and separated by a deep gully from, the central buttress. To get this photograph I tied the ropes off, raced round to the head of Kilt Rock, then raced back to re-belay Bob.

OPPOSITE: A large boulder, all that is left of a column of dolerite, rests on the underlying Jurassic limestone on the beach at Staffin Slip. Even in winter, this cove can provide a wonderful sun trap in which to take refuge and watch the seabirds.

BELOW: A croft and outhouses above Staffin Bay. Traditional crofts, constructed from local materials, are in perfect proportion to their surroundings. The Quirang stands high above.

OVERLEAF: This image, taken with a long lens, is from the east coast road above Uig, looking out to the distant snow-clad mountains of Harris in the Outer Hebrides. Such is the clarity that it looks as if you can reach out and touch the distant hills, which are in fact some 40km away. The highest mountain is An Clisearm (799m).

BELOW: Looking south down the North Ridge to the distinctive mountain of Beinn Edra.

OPPOSITE: The Staffin–Uig Pass is steep and exciting in any conditions – in snow, doubly so. This is the Staffin side of the pass; the flat-topped pyramid beyond is Cleat.

OVERLEAF: As a gaggle of geese circle above me, checking out their intended landing point on Loch Mealt, the half-light of winter adds a dramatic touch to this view towards the North Ridge of Trotternish. To the far left lies the Storr while near the right edge of the image can be seen the truncated cone of Sgurr a' Mhadaidh Ruaidh (the Peak of the Red Fox).

people and culture

OPPOSITE: The Isle of Skye Pipe Band in full flow in the centre of Portree, with its stirring marches and ceremonial pomp, is a fine spectacle which never fails to draw crowds. Many traditional activities, along with piping and pipe bands, are celebrated during the annual Skye Games, held at Portree around the first week in August.

People of the Western Isles have a lovely soft, lilting way of speaking English and a kindness of heart that is surely born from rising above adversity. Perhaps the hard realities of earning a living from the elemental landscape and extremes of weather have shaped them thus.

At the time of writing, the resident population of Skye is around 10,000 people, a number that swells considerably with the influx of tourists during the summer months. Around half of the island people speak Gaelic, and are proud of their traditions and language. There is now a Gaelic University at Sleat, Sabhal Mor Ostaig, intent on keeping the language alive and flourishing. Music, art and fun are an important part of the culture of Skye and impromptu ceilidhs, gatherings of people to celebrate in word and music, remain a facet of life. Perhaps the best-known modern Gaelic poet, Sorley MacLean (1911–96), was born on Raasay and lived much of his life on Skye.

I well remember the first time I climbed on Kilt Rock. Ignorant of the proper approach, I found myself in the corner of a field with a barbed wire fence separating me from the top of the cliff. Suddenly a farmer appeared and quickly approached. My immediate instinct was that I was going to be told, in unequivocal terms, to go back to the road and try again. Much to my relief and surprise, he simply asked if I was heading for Kilt Rock, then took off his jacket, laid it across the barbed wire and helped me over. Such is the nature of the people of Skye.

The Skye Bridge, providing a physical link with the island and mainland Scotland, was opened in 1995; it is said that it is so tall in order to allow the royal yacht *Britannia* (now defunct) to sail beneath. It was built under a private finance initiative, and the tolls that were imposed met with widespread opposition. The protest was led by the pressure group SKAT (Skye and Kyle Against Tolls) which triumphed on 21 December 2004 when the Scottish Executive purchased the bridge from its owners, and the tolls were dropped.

RIGHT: Bill Cowie, property manager and wildlife expert, is responsible for the converted holiday cottages on the small island of Rona, north of Raasay off the east coast of Trotternish. He is holding a set of Rona's own stamps, which can be used in the one postbox on the island – weekly collections of mail and people when weather and tide permit. Rona once had a healthy community, but by 1922 it had dwindled to 100 people, at which point most of them, lacking any government support, decided to leave. The crofts fell into ruin until, in 1993, the island was bought from the Scottish Secretary by Dorte Jensen. The Jensen Foundation has since invested, rebuilt and refurbished a number of properties; today, Rona has become a much sought-after back-to-nature holiday destination, with self-catering crofts of a high standard.

ABOVE: On Skye the sea is still the great provider. Lobster creeling is one of the main fishing activites around the coast; fine specimens such as this are whisked off by air to the great restaurants of the world.

LEFT: Squid, occasionally brought up in a lobster creel, are returned to the sea none the worse for their adventure.

RIGHT: Lifting lobster pots below Ben Chracaig and MacCoitir's Cave, outside Portree Harbour.

BELOW: The attractive, bustling harbour of Portree retains great character and charm, with a mixture of fishing boats and pleasure craft, along with a permanent lifeboat station.

climbing and mountaineering

BELOW: The infamous Bad Step, which must be negotiated when following the coastal path from Camasunary (and the Elgol road) to Loch Coruisk. If the crack rising diagonally from the bottom right is followed, for climbers it is a straightforward outing. For those who do not climb or who lose the line, it can be troublesome. I know one Skye man, on a sponsored run for charity in early spring, who slipped and slid down the rock directly into the sea at high tide; there was no back-up and no one else was around. Having survived the fall, he had to swim to shore, then continue his long, lonely and cold journey back to the Sligachan Hotel through the wilds of the Black Cuillin.

With its many magnificent mountains and steep places, Skye has a rich climbing history. Mountaineering in the Black Cuillin hills began in the early part of the nineteenth century with the first significant ascent, of Sgurr nan Gillean, in 1836. This tremendous peak fell to Professor James Forbes who had hired the guiding services of a talented local Skye man, Duncan MacIntyre, to accomplish the ascent. Their route is now known as the Tourist Route, although the name is misleading, for there is an awkward and exposed corner to climb before the top block can be gained. Despite almost two hundred years of climbing, new routes are still being climbed in the Black Cuillin with the last cutting-edge route Skye Wall, on Coir–Uisg Buttress above the head of Loch Coruisk, recorded by Dave Birkett and Alan Steele in 2007.

Alexander Nicholson, later to become Sheriff, was born on Skye and was a pioneer of a number of new routes in the Black Cuillin. Along with Angus Macrae, a local shepherd, he made the first ascent in 1873 of the highest peak. He thought it might be called Scur-a-Laghain, though it is now known as Sgurr Alasdair. In the 1880s, development began to take off in a big way when the Alpinists turned their attentions away from Europe to focus on Skye.

Skye man John Mackenzie was at the centre of much of this activity. He had a great affinity for climbing, having soloed Sgurr nan Gillean at the age of ten, and naturally set himself up as mountain guide to the Cuillin. He took the brothers Charles and Lawrence Pilkington to the foot of the Inaccessible Pinnacle, and watched while they made the first ascent. The next year, he took off his shoes and soloed it – he didn't possess climbing boots! Various parts of the ridge were traversed, the individual tops rapidly fell, and numerous climbs and different ways were discovered.

In 1888, John Mackenzie met the great Norman Collie, a leading scientist and one of Britain's finest mountaineers. They

formed a lifetime partnership which lasted until Mackenzie's death in 1933. Inseparable in life, they now lie next to each other in the graveyard of the Free Presbyterian Church of Struan.

In 1896, the Scottish Mountaineering Club (SMC) was formally constituted. Many members were active and the club was the first to begin to keep accurate records of the peaks and climbs of the Cuillin. In the same year, the last unclimbed peak in the Cuillin (the last unclimbed peak in Britain), the north top of Sgurr Coir an Lochan, was finally vanquished. In the last year of the century, another event took place that is still remembered with some incredulity. In the Red Cuillin, Havildar Harkabir

Thapa, a Gurkha soldier, ran to the summit of Glamaig and back to the Sligachan Hotel in 55 minutes – in bare feet!

The early 1900s saw a good deal of serious rock climbing development, with some mind-boggling routes tackling the great unclimbed faces of the Cuillin, notably the 305m Sron na Ciche above Glen Brittle. High amid a sea of rock which constitutes the face of Sron na Ciche, the protruding block of the Cioch (the Breast) was climbed by Collie and Mackenzie in 1906. This was some seven years after Collie had first identified this remarkable feature, by observing the dark shadow it cast on the otherwise evenly sunlit slabs. The following year, H. Holden and Ashley Abraham climbed the superb Cioch Direct following a steep natural line directly up to the top of the Cioch from the base of the crag below. Abraham's influential book *Rock Climbing in Skye* was published in 1908, with the result that development of climbing in Skye took off massively.

It continues unabated to this day and it is beyond the scope of this brief summary to include all but a few exploits. The first continuous traverse of the Main Cuillin Ridge was made by Leslie Shadbolt and Alastair McLaren in 1911. In 1918 D. R. Pye and Shadbolt added to Sron na Ciche the evocatively named Crack of Doom! Noel Odell moved to the Red Cuillin to make an ascent of the nose of Marsco in 1943. I. Allen climbed the wild and bold slab of Arrow Route in 1944 – it remains virtually protection-free even with all of today's high-tech gear.

The Creagh Dhu Climbing Club did great things in the 1950s and early 1960s – notably Hamish McInnes, Patsy Walsh (whose powerful Trophy Crack compared in difficulty with anything climbed in Britain at that time) and Johnnie Cunningham. I hope the many I have missed will accept my apologies. Ian Clough climbed the inaccessible – it's out at sea – stack of the Old Lady, the largest of MacLeod's Maidens, in 1959. Tom Patey joined forces with Chris Bonington in 1960 to produce, most famously, the delectable King Cobra on the

remote Loch Coruisk side of Sgurr Mhic Choinnich. One of the least known and most difficult routes of that period was Robin Smith's Thunder Rib on the North-West Face of Sgurr a' Mhadaidh. Its description in the SMC guidebook of the era is an absolute classic of understatement, running something like: 'Thunder Rib, 1000ft, Exceptionally Severe. Start at the bottom of the rib and climb the line of least resistance'!

Moving on, the route of the 1970s was undoubtedly Mick Fowler's inspirational Stairway to Heaven, taking the centre of the face of Bla Bheinn's Great Prow.

Latterly, climbing development has expanded a long way beyond the Black Cuillin, principally on to the tremendous sea cliffs that punctuate the coastline. The first serious route to break away from the Cuillin was the landmark ascent of the Old Man of Storr by Don Whillans in 1956. This was followed by a trickle of others, until Ed Grindley climbed Supercharger on Neist Point in 1981. This route opened the floodgates to the massive untapped potential of the Skye sea cliffs, and was followed by the development of Kilt Rock in 1983. The cliffs of Staffin, Flodigarry and the awesome Rubha Hunish were all climbed in rapid succession.

Skye, whatever the weather, will always be a favourite place to climb. There really is nowhere else quite like it. As Ashley Abraham wrote in *Rock Climbing in Skye*:

> Besides, it should be borne in mind that Skye is preferred to Switzerland by many climbers who are intimate with both districts. I count myself amongst these. My memories of the Coolin are more pleasurable and lasting than those of the Alps. . . . Many there are who would rather forgo for ever Switzerland than Skye; few there be who have once been there but have returned again, in spite of the journey!

BELOW: The late Freddy Snallam on the classic, appropriately named, Crack of Doom on the huge cliff of Sron na Ciche. First climbed by D. R. Pye and Leslie Shadbolt in 1918, it was brought to wider attention by Bill Murray's wonderfully evocative account in Mountaineering In Scotland (1947), one of the finest books ever written on climbing, penned from memory, on toilet paper, while Murray was a prisoner-of-war in Germany.

RIGHT: My companion of many Skye adventures, John Hargreaves, on the narrow rock ledge across the face of Sgurr Mhic Choinnich on the Coire Lagan side, on our first traverse of the main ridge in May 1988. The ledge was pioneered by Norman Collie and is known today as Collie's Ledge. He wrote: 'It is the individuality of the Cuillin that makes the lover of the hills come back again and again to Skye.'

index

Illustration captions in italics

Abraham, Ashley 54, 125, 126
Act of Council (1360) 10
Act of Settlement (1701) 19
Alexander III 10
Allen, I. 125
Allt Coir a' Mhadaidh 70
Allt na Cille 18
Am Basteir 11, 62, 81
An Coileach 33
An Diallaid 81
An t-Aigeach 86
Anne, Queen 19
Ardtrek 11
Ardmore Bay 18
Ardnamurchan 21
Armadale 7, 10
Ascrib Islands 15

Balmeanach 90
Battle of the Braes 22
Beaker People 16–18
Bealach 20
Bealach a' Garbh-choire 65
Bealach Beag 103
Bealach Beiste 30
Beinn Dearg 30, 32, 34, 44
Beinn Dearg Mheadhonach 32, 34, 44
Beinn Dearg Mhor 30, 34, 41, 44
Beinn Edra 90, 102, 116
Beinn na Caillich 10, 25, 43
Beinn na Cro 41
Beinn Staic 81
Ben Aslak 10
Ben Chracaig 123
Ben Suardal 10, 84
Ben Tianavaig 90
Ben Volovaig 94, 105
Bhasteir Tooth 11, 62, 81
Birkett, Dave 15, 124, 126
Bla Bheinn 10, 24, 25, 28, 29, 34, 38, 45, 51, 126
Black Cuillin 4, 7, 11, 24, 39, 40, 45, 52, 53, 54–83, 84, 90, 124, 126
Bonington, Chris 125
Bonnie Prince Charlie 7, 8, 10, 14, 15, 18, 19–20
Boreag 10, 21
Boswell, James 20
Bracadale 11
Braes 22
Broadford 7, 10, 11, 21, 24, 34, 43
Bruach na Frithe 69, 72, 80
Bun-idein 94
Burke, Betty 20

Cain, Ginger 69
Caisteal Maol 10
Camasunary 24, 40, 124
Carbost 11, 72
Charles I of England 19
Charles II of England 19
Ciche na Bheinne Deirge 34
Cill Chriosad 10, 21
Cioch 64, 125
Clach Glas 24, 25, 28, 29, 38, 45, 51
Clachan 15

Clearances, Highland 10, 12, 18, 21–22
Cleat 116
Clough, Ian 125
Coir a' Ghrunnda 65
Coir an Eich 80, 81
Coire a' Bhasteir 63
Coire a' Ghreadaidh 80
Coire Lagan 11, 64, 127
Coire na Banachdich 81
Coire na Creiche 70, 80
Collie, Norman 54, 64, 124, 125, 127
Coral Beaches 12
Cowie, Bill 120
Cowie, Ross 12
Crab, Davie 53
Creag a' Lain 90
Creagh Dhu Climbing Club 125
Cuchullin 44
Culloden, Battle of (1746) 15, 18, 20, 21
Cumberland, Duke of ('the Butcher') 20
Cunningham, Johnnie 125

Druim na Ruaige 32
Druim nan Ramh 40, 54
Drynoch River 87
Duirinish 7, 12, 18, 22, 52, 84, 86, 89
Dun Akyn 10
Dun Beag 12, 16, 18, 89
Dun Caan 11
Dun Gerashader 18
Dun Skudiburgh 18
Dunscaith 44
Duntulm 15, 20, 90, 100, 108
Dunvegan 8, 11, 12, 16

Eas a' Bhradain 49
Eilean Ban 8, 10
Eilean Glas 86
Eilean Ruairidh 44
Elgol 10, 18, 21, 24, 25, 34, 55, 76, 124
Elishader 14, 90, 91

Fairy Glen 91
Fictan Dearg 43
Fionn Corrie 80
Fiskavaig 18
Flodigarry 14, 52, 86, 90, 98, 126
Forbes, James 124
Fowler, Mick 126

Gars-bheinn 24, 28, 30, 38, 54, 55, 76
George II of England 20
Glamaig 11, 24, 25, 30, 32, 33, 45, 50, 80, 125
Glasnakille 10, 18, 24
Gleann Beag 18
Glen Arroch 10
Glen Brittle 8, 11, 12, 52, 54, 60, 70, 72, 76, 81, 125
Glen Drynoch 89
Glen Sligachan 7, 11, 24, 25, 40, 43, 52, 54
Glendale 12, 22
Glendale Martyrs 12, 22
Glenelg 10, 18
Glorious Revolution (1688) 19
Grindley, Ed 14, 126

Haakon IV of Norway 10, 19
Hargreaves, John 94, 127
Harta Corrie 40, 68, 69
Healabhal Bheag 12, 18
Healabhal Mhor 12, 18
Holden, H. 125

Idrigill 12
Inner Sound 7

James IV 19
James VI (and I) 19
James VII (and II) 19
Jensen Foundation (Rona) 120
Johnson, Dr Samuel 15, 20, 21

Kilmuir 15
Kilt Rock 14, 52, 53, 90, 94, 96, 110, 120, 126
Kintail 10
Kyle Akin 8, 10
Kyle of Lochalsh 7, 8
Kyleakin 7, 8, 10
Kylerhea 7

Largs, Battle of (1263) 10
Lee, Alastair (Posing Productions) 126
Leventon, Charlie 8
Loch Ainort 11, 24, 34, 44, 49
Loch an Fhir 76
Loch an Fhir-bhallaich 76
Loch Brittle 16
Loch Bracadale 12
Loch Cill Chriosad 49
Loch Coruisk 4, 10–11, 40, 54, 55, 58, 86, 124, 126
Loch Dunvegan 89
Loch Eishort 44
Loch Harport 11, 80
Loch Mealt 14, 90, 116
Loch na Cuilce 86
Loch nan Eilean 72
Loch Poolteil 22
Loch Portree 85
Loch Scavaig 4, 10, 24, 54, 58
Loch Sligachan 11, 24
Loch Slapin 10, 24, 25, 28, 34, 38, 41, 44, 45
Loch Sneosdal 19
Loch Snizort 15, 16, 18, 100
Lochan Dubha 24
Lon nan Earb 19
Lord of The Isles 19
Lota Corrie 69
Lower Breakish 43
Luib 34

MacCoitir's Cave 123
MacDonald, Flora 8, 14, 15, 20, 21
MacDonald, Hugh 20
MacDonalds 18, 19, 20, 22, 100
McInnes, Hamish 53, 125
MacIntyre, Duncan 124
Mackenzie, John 64, 124, 125
MacKenzie, Tommy 12
Mackinnons of Strath 10
McLaren, Alastair 54, 125
MacLean, Sorley 22, 54, 120
MacLeod, John 54
MacLeod, Willie 107, 108
MacLeods 12, 18, 19, 20, 54
Macleod's Maidens 12, 125
Macleod's Tables 12, 18
Macpherson, John (Glendale Martyr) 22

Macrae, Angus 124
Mallaig 7, 10
Marsco 24, 25, 29, 32, 34, 38, 40, 43, 51, 125
Martin, Martin (Mhartainn MacGill Mhartainn) 20
Maxwell, Gavin 8, 10
Meall a' Mhaoil 24
Meall na Suiramach 14, 90
Mealt waterfall 14, 53
Minginish 7, 11, 18
Moonen Bay 84
Murray, Bill 127
Murray, Lord George 20

Napier, Lord 22
Neist Point 12, 84, 86, 126
Nicholson, Alexander 124
Nicholsons 18

Odell, Noel 43, 125
Old Man of Storr 12, 14, 90, 100, 126
Orbost 12
Oronsay 12

Pabay 43
Patey, Tom 53, 125
Pennant, Thomas 43
Perth, Treaty of (1266) 10
Pictish Symbol Stone 15, 18
Pilkington, Charles 124
Pilkington, Lawrence 124
Pinnacle 11, 60, 62, 63, 124
Port an Luig Mhoir 10
Portnalong 80
Portree 7, 8, 11, 12, 15, 16, 22, 33, 39, 53, 89, 90, 120, 123
'Psyche' (DVD) 126
Pye, D. R. 127

Quirang 14, 84, 90, 91, 102, 113

Raasay 11, 14, 30, 120
Red Cuillin 7, 8, 10, 11, 24–51, 52, 65, 80, 84, 90, 124, 125
Robertson, Brian 53
Rona 14, 120
Ross, Dugald 14
Royal Commission (under Napier) 22
Rubh an Dunain 16
Rubha Hunish 15, 52, 86, 90, 94, 104, 105, 107, 108, 125, 126
Rubha nan Clach 11

Sabhal Mor Ostaig (University of Gaelic) 10, 120
St Columba's Island 18
Scalpay 43
Sconser 11, 90
Scott, Walter 11
Scottish Mountaineering Club (SMC) 124
Sgurr a' Bhasteir 62, 81
Sgurr a' Ghreadaidh 11, 58, 72
Sgurr a' Mhadaidh 11, 126
Sgurr a' Mhadaidh Ruaidh 116
Sgurr Alasdair 11, 54, 65, 124
Sgurr an Fheadain 70
Sgurr Coir an Lochan 124
Sgurr Dearg 11, 81
Sgurr Dubh Beag 58
Sgurr Mhairi 32, 33, 50
Sgurr Mhic Choinnich 126, 127
Sgurr na Banachdich 80, 81
Sgurr na Bhairnich 69

Sgurr na Coinnich 10
Sgurr na Stri 4, 54, 58
Sgurr nan Each 28, 65
Sgurr nan Eag 65
Sgurr nan Gillean 11, 52, 54, 55, 60, 62, 65, 72, 81, 124
Sgurr nan Gobhar 80, 81
Sgurr Sgumain 65
Shadbolt, Leslie 54, 125, 127
Sheehan, Andrew 125
Shiel Bridge 10
SKAT (Skye and Kyle Against Tolls) 8, 120
Skeabost 16, 18, 89
'Skye Boat Song' 7, 14, 15
Skye Bridge 8, 120
Skye Games 12
Skye Museum of Island Life, Kilmuir 15
Sleat 7, 10, 44, 76, 120
Sligachan Hotel 8, 11, 24, 32, 33, 34, 38, 39, 49, 54, 72, 81, 124, 125
Smith, Robin 126
Snallam, Freddy 127
Snizort River 16, 18
Soay 10, 54
Spar Cave 10, 24
Sron na Ciche 11, 60, 64, 72, 76, 125, 127
Sron Vourlin 90, 102
Staffin 14, 16, 52, 85, 86, 90, 91, 98, 99, 113, 116, 126
Staffin Museum 14
Staffin–Uig Pass 14, 90, 91, 116
Statutes of Icolmkill (1609) 19
Steele, Alan 124, 126
Steer, Luke 84
Stein 12
Storr 12, 14, 18, 90, 91, 100, 103, 107, 116, 126
Strath 10
Strath Beag 41
Strath Mor 41
Strath na Creitheach 24
Strath Suardal 10, 21, 24, 84
Strathaird 7, 10, 11, 21, 24–51, 58, 84
Strathaird 7, 10, 11, 21, 24–51, 58, 84
Struan 11, 18, 124
Struanmore 16
Stuart dynasty 19; *see also* Bonnie Prince Charlie
Suardal 21
Suisinish 10, 21

Talisker 11
Thapa, Havildar Harkabir 124–5
Torrin 10, 24, 34
Tote 15, 18
Treaty of Union (1707) 19
Trotternish 7, 8, 12, 14, 15, 16, 18, 19, 20, 39, 52, 84, 85, 90–119, 120
Trumpan 12, 18
Tulm Bay 100
Turner, J. M. W. 11

Uig 7, 8, 15, 90, 91, 113
Ullinish 12, 18

Walsh, Patsy 12, 125
Waternish 7, 12, 15, 18, 89, 100
Whillans, Don 12, 126
Wightman, Bob 110
William of Orange, and Mary 19